Archangels

A Spiritual Guide to Connecting with an Archangel, Guardian Angels, and Spirit Guides along with Tuning into Angelic Protection

Your Free Gift (only available for a limited time)

Thanks for getting this book! If you want to learn more about various spirituality topics, then join Mari Silva's community and get a free guided meditation MP3 for awakening your third eye. This guided meditation mp3 is designed to open and strengthen ones third eye so you can experience a higher state of consciousness. Simply visit the link below the image to get started.

https://spiritualityspot.com/meditation

Contents

INTRODUCTION 1

CHAPTER ONE: INTRODUCTION TO SPIRIT GUIDES 3

SPIRIT GUIDES...4

KINDS OF SPIRIT GUIDES 5

YOUR SPIRIT GUIDES' ROLES...8

CHAPTER TWO: WHO ARE THE ANGELS AND ARCHANGELS? 11

WHERE ANGELS COME FROM 11

HOW MANY ANGELS EXIST?...12

PERSONALITIES 12

RANKINGS...12

THE ARCHANGELS...13

ARCHANGELS IN ZOROASTRIANISM 14

ARCHANGELS IN JUDAISM 15

ARCHANGELS IN EASTERN ORTHODOX TRADITION 17

ARCHANGELS IN PROTESTANTISM 18

ARCHANGELS IN OCCULTIST TRADITIONS..18

CHAPTER THREE: THE ARCHANGELS OF THE FOUR
DIRECTIONS..19

ARCHANGEL MICHAEL 19

ARCHANGEL GABRIEL 24

ARCHANGEL RAPHAEL 27

Archangel Uriel 31

CHAPTER FOUR: MEETING YOUR GUARDIAN ANGEL..........................35

Facts about Guardian Angels 35

How to Reach Out to Your Guardian Angels 36

Signs Your Guardian Angels Are around You............................. 38

I've Noticed My Angels...Now What? 40

CHAPTER FIVE: ANGELS AND ASTROLOGY 42

The Seven Archangels of the Week... 42

Angels and Zodiac Signs.. 43

CHAPTER SIX: HOW TO INVOKE AN ANGEL.........................50

Prayers to Summon Your Angel.. 50

Prayer to Your Guardian Angel... 52

Tips for Connecting with Angels... 53

CHAPTER SEVEN: ANGELIC SIGNS TO LOOK OUT FOR 58

CHAPTER EIGHT: TUNING INTO ANGELIC PROTECTION 65

Visualizing a Protective Light Shield.. 66

Everyday Protection 66

Protection for Kids... 67

Protection against Bad Luck.. 67

Protection against Gossip, Slander, and Plots against You 67

No Shortcuts... 68

How to Boost Your Connection with Angels 68

Michael's Sigil for Protection 70

CHAPTER NINE: WORKING WITH MICHAEL AND GABRIEL 72

Working with Michael.. 72

Working with Archangel Gabriel 76

CHAPTER TEN: WORKING WITH RAPHAEL AND URIEL.....................79

Working with Archangel Raphael.. 79

Working with Uriel 83

CHAPTER ELEVEN: WORKING WITH ARIEL AND AZRAEL.................87

Working with Archangel Ariel 87

Working with Archangel Azrael 90

CHAPTER TWELVE: HOW TO CONTACT OTHER SPIRIT GUIDES 96

SPIRIT GUIDE MEDITATION...100

COMMUNICATING WITH OTHER SPIRITS WITH YOUR GUIDES'
PROTECTION 102

CONCLUSION..105

HERE'S ANOTHER BOOK BY MARI SILVA THAT YOU MIGHT
LIKE...107

YOUR FREE GIFT (ONLY AVAILABLE FOR A LIMITED TIME) 108

REFERENCES 109

Introduction

What would you do if you could have divine assistance in whatever you wanted? How much easier would your life be? Do you need protection, provision, promotion, or anything else? How great would it be to know you can always call on someone very dependable, and they'll get the job done for you? What if you could connect with loved ones that have passed on and gain invaluable insight and guidance from the other side? How does it feel to know that you're never alone, even when it seems like it? Well, you're about to find out about all that and more.

In this book, you're going to learn about divine beings and spirit guides. By the time you're through, you will have all the tools you need to establish a direct connection with the archangels, angels, and spirit guides assigned to you. You may not be aware of them now, but the truth is they've always been with you. Now, you're about to create a powerful and beneficial connection between you and divinity.

Unlike other books on the subject, this one is very easy to read and understand. If you're new to the idea of connecting with the spirit world, you don't need to feel overwhelmed or frightened. This book will take you by the hand and walk you through everything you need to know on the topic of angels, archangels, and more. You'll be able to work with the concepts presented on these pages even if you're a beginner. You will have such undeniable results that you'll know for a fact your life will never be the same again.

You're going to get very clear instructions on how to reach out to each archangel and how they can help you with whatever it is you might have struggled with your whole life. We all have that one thing that has continued to plague us. Maybe it has been that way since birth, or it only cropped up recently, but it feels like you could never fix it. You might have tried talking to friends, your religious head, your therapist, and even your pet rock. Yet, no one has been able to help you out of the trouble you're facing. It feels almost like you're doomed. Here's the thing: It doesn't have to be that way.

There are beings whose very mission is to take care of all of life. You, dear reader, are a part of life. That means you have access to these beings as well. The trouble is that no one taught us how to reach out to them, tune in, and hear what they have to say. We're taught to do addition well, spell correctly, and know the difference between rectangles and parallelograms. But society doesn't think it is important to learn how to draw on the power of spirit to live richer, fuller lives on earth. I hope that with this book, you will learn of the assistance that has been available to you all along. Not only that, but I also want you to know exactly how to foster the relationship between you and divinity. This way, you will live the reality of these words written by the prophet Isaiah:"...*before they call, I will answer; and while they are yet speaking, I will hear.*"

Chapter One: Introduction to Spirit Guides

You didn't come to this world alone. Even on days when you've felt so alone, rejected, and unloved, there was someone there with you, though you may not have realized it. On your happiest days, they're right there with you, cheering you on. On your not-so-great days, they're there anyway, loving you with no judgment. They're always sending you messages to help you find your way, feel better, work through a problem, or cheer you on. They don't care that you've made bad decisions. You may beat yourself up, but they would never do that. They'll send you a message in any way they can to let you know that it is okay and it is not the end.

I remember one evening after a very rough day I'd had at work. All in one day, I'd just been scammed, told that the little restaurant I worked at would be shut down, and dumped over the phone via text message. At the time, I had no friends, no family to turn to, no one but my then significant other, who had just made it clear in a two-word text that they were done being significant to me. As I headed home after a long day of working on my feet, feeling scared, hurt, and alone, I had some of the darkest thoughts take over my mind. Somehow, the pain was so much it moved me to mutter a little prayer, "Please just give me a sign that everything will be okay. Please..."

I wasn't particularly religious, and I had no idea why I even said that, as though someone was listening. However, a curious thing happened as soon as I said that: someone got on the bus wearing a Liverpool football shirt. He smiled at me as he walked past. For some reason, I craned my neck to look, and there on the back of his shirt were the words, "You'll Never Walk Alone." That wasn't the first time I'd seen it, I'll tell you that, but it was the first time it hit me so deeply. It was as if all the air was sucked out of my lungs, and time stood still, and I felt a comforting warmth wash over me along with goosebumps. Now, you could dismiss that as a coincidence, except when I got home thirty minutes later, I walked past someone in the hallway singing — you guessed it — "You'll never walk alone." I was, for the second time that evening, covered in goosebumps.

At that moment, I decided I would try to interact with whoever was so obviously trying to communicate with me. I just wanted to know what my fate was. I turned on the radio and caught the tail end of a song that said, "Everything works out in the end." Needless to say, it did.

Spirit Guides

Spirit guides. Everyone's got at least one. It doesn't matter if you believe they exist or not, and fortunately, they're not offended by your lack of belief. Spirit guides are spiritual beings who help you, guide you, and keep you safe. They provide you with positive energy when you're feeling low. They gently nudge you where you need to go to achieve your purpose. Spirit guides have unique roles to play and can help you in all aspects of your life.

Kinds of Spirit Guides

Seven kinds of spirit guides can help you out with the business of living.

Ancestors are spirit guides connected to you by your spiritual or genetic lineage. They could either be beloved ones you knew who have passed on or family from previous generations. You may not know them at all, but they know you. They could also be your spiritual family. It is more usual to connect with ancestors from many generations back.

They offer you their support and guidance in multiple ways. They can help you with limiting beliefs, generational fears, and trauma. They can help you to heal, even when it feels like you'll forever be wounded. They could also help you with regular, everyday things.

Your ancestors can act as teacher guides, showing you the ropes in a new endeavor or helping you deal with difficult situations. They could also help you discover the mental and spiritual gifts you have within you and teach you how to flow better with life.

Angels are spiritual entities of the angelic hierarchy. They can act as spiritual guides or messengers. Among them are Guardian Angels and Archangels, who work directly with us earthlings. They can communicate to you through others, a line of a song, a conversation between two strangers that you overhear a snippet of, your gut, or your dreams. They work to keep you moving in a direction that will serve your highest good in this incarnation and the others to come.

Your guardian angel is the one assigned to you from birth, charged with the task of supporting you all through your days. They are fully aware of your mission on earth. They know what the end game is for you, and they do all they can to help you stay the course. They know your strengths and what you struggle with. They lead you on your way to expressing your ultimate Truth so that you can live authentically.

You've no doubt heard of angels thanks to one religion or the other. The thing about angels, though, is that they aren't religious. Regardless of your faith, gender, status, or beliefs, they are there for you and will guide you unconditionally. Think of your guardian angel as your ultimate best friend who can lead you to amazing places in life when you deliberately acknowledge and interact with them. Suppose you want to get in touch with angels and archangels. In that case, you should first cultivate a relationship with your personal guide.

Archangels are also angelic, and they offer humans help, too. They're charged to work with larger groups, but that doesn't mean you cannot call on them when you need help with a matter that is their forte. Of all the archangels, Michael is one of the most popular. We'll learn more about these wonderful beings later in this book.

Star Beings are like your galactic family. They work to take care of humanity, and in particular, *Starseed souls.* Starseed souls originated from higher dimensions of life and star systems like Lyra, Andromeda, Sirius, the Pleiades, and more. You may have known these beings in a past life, or you'll meet them in the future in a different star system.

They work to help humans evolve. Their goal is the evolution of the soul. So, they guide you on the path of ascension as they've walked this path themselves and know how to get us to our destination in the most effective way possible.

Ascended Masters are those beings who have lived on earth for many different incarnations, and that makes them masters of the business of living. They can serve as teacher guides, helping you learn what you must so you can ascend just like they have. Seeing as they've been human in the past, they know what it is like to feel how you do. They deeply understand your challenges, whether physical or emotional. Therefore, their guidance can be very powerful when you choose to follow it. Some include Jesus or Yeshua, Merlin, Mother Mary, Babaji, Sanat Kumara, Saint Germain, Melchizedek, Maitreya, Quan Yin, etc.

Animal Spirit Guides are also called Totems or Power Animals. They show up as animals and help us in life, healing, inspiring, and supporting us when times are hard. Their primary role is to help you be your best self on earth, which means aligning with the earth's energies. They help you remain grounded. These guides can empower you and are full of magic and wisdom.

Animal spirit guides like the vulture, snake, or jaguar can move between the spiritual and physical worlds. They can also help you pierce the veil that divides both worlds to develop your relationship with the spirit. Other kinds of animal spirit guides can help you master your fears. They can protect you, give you wisdom, and imbue you with their attributes as needed.

Goddesses and Gods are Divine spiritual beings. Their personalities and origin stories are vibrant, and they have traits that represent aspects of Divine Life Force. They make it easier for us to connect with Divinity on a more personal level. Usually, they are beings that once used to be physical themselves, in a different epoch. They inhabit the spirit realm now and are allies who can teach us how to navigate our physical lives.

To be clear, they do not represent the ultimate Source itself. These beings simply make it easier for us humans to connect with the divine as they manifest various aspects of Source Energy. They show up across cultures, traditions, and eras. They're known as devas, divinities, heroes, and sometimes immortals. You could have an affinity for gods and goddesses of your own tradition. You may be more drawn to those from a parallel or past life. The goddesses and gods include Idemili, Osun, Lakshmi, Odin, Horus, Ra, Thoth, Yemoja, Ganesha, Hathor, Ogun, Amadioha, and more.

Elemental Spirit Guides or elementals dwell in one of the four classical elements — earth, air, fire, or water. Not all of them are benevolent, but the ones that are can be considered as spirit guides. There are four major kinds of elementals. *Gnomes* are earth elementals; **undines** are water elementals; **pyraustas** or **salamanders** are ether and fire elementals, while **Sylphs** are air elementals.

If you're in tune with nature, you might sense a connection to these beings who dwell in lakes, trees, streams, mountains, and even lava fields. You can develop this connection to receive guidance and assistance from these guides and work with the wisdom of nature.

These beings belong to the Faery Realm, which is also called the Middle Kingdom. Other than elementals, other beings inhabit the astral and etheric realms and help humanity. Nature sprites, tree elves, flower faeries, and malevolent elementals are formed from negative emotions and thoughts.

Your Spirit Guides' Roles

Life Guides are in charge of our entire team of guides. Your life guides have been with you from the day you were born. They'll be there even in death. They work to coordinate with every other guide you have assigned to your life. One of them works as your guardian angel. This doesn't mean other angels or beings can't act as your guardian angel, though.

Timing Guides are the ones who handle synchronicity. In other words, they make sure you're at the right place, at the right time. They'll connect you to the right people, places, events, and things under the right circumstances. It is possible to have something you've always wanted show up at the wrong time and prove more a nuisance than a pleasure. These are the guides that help keep things going according to the Divine schedule.

Teaching Guides are responsible for guiding you along your life path, teaching you the important lessons you need to grow and develop physically and spiritually. They can show up in various forms depending on the goals or the lessons you need to learn. They can guide you through your meditation and dreams. Usually, they leave signs for you to follow, to reassure you that you're on the right path, or get you to take a different one that would serve your highest good.

Creativity Guides are responsible for helping you with creative work. They're the ones that nudge you to dream and dream big. They connect you with your innate talents. If you suspect there might be things you're good at that you haven't discovered yet, call on them for assistance, and they'll reveal all you need to know. Just keep your eyes and mind open for their signs and messages.

Karmic Guides can help you work out your collective and personal karma so that you can shed the chains that hold you back and finally get off the wheel. When you resolve all your karma, you can move on to the next level of soul expression.

Astral Guides are the ones who help you out when you visit the heavenly realm. They teach you how to leave your body. If you ask them, they can help your astral body leave your physical one when it feels stuck. They can also make you feel safe in an understandably strange world when you're new to astral projection. If you need to find your way around the astral realm or seek guidance on a physical matter, enlist the help of your astral guides.

Protection Guides are pretty much like bodyguards. They keep you safe physically, spiritually, mentally, and emotionally, but that all comes down to your intentions and what you allow. These guides stay with their wards from birth to death, and they are very enlightened beings. They keep you safe from spiritual influences and entities that do not have your best interests at heart and keep you from making choices that will lead to your destruction.

Joy Guides are very childlike and playful. They love nothing but to help you find joy in everything. When you feel heavy or down, they find ways to make you crack a smile. If you want to connect with them more, let them know, and make laughter a priority in your life.

Ascension Guides have one goal: To help you ascend spiritually. They act and intervene when they must lead you down a path that will end with you advancing in spirit.

Helper Guides aren't always with you. Depending on what you're working on, they come and go. If you're learning some new skill, the helper guides who have experience in that space will show up and teach you what you need to know. If you decide to do something else, those helpers will be replaced by the more knowledgeable ones in that field. They can also act as healers or as a compass when you feel lost about what to do. They'll show you what is yours and what you should release.

Chapter Two: Who Are the Angels and Archangels?

Angels are divine beings that dwell in the spirit realm who have more power than humans. The spirit realm is where most things take place before they manifest here on earth, so it only makes sense that angels already know the best course of action for you to take to get you where you want to go.

Where Angels Come From

Most people view angels as taught by Western Christianity. This perspective, however, most likely has its roots in Zoroastrianism. This ancient Persian religious system was prominent from 559 BC to 651 BC, when the Persian empire was at its highest. Zoroastrianism was, by all accounts, the world's most powerful religion in Christ's lifetime. Of the monotheist religions, it is one of the most ancient. Even to this day, it is still in practice, particularly in India and Iran. Suffice it to say that across religions, you can deduce that the angels were created by the supreme being, in a time before time, before the world ever was.

How Many Angels Exist?

Other than the seven archangels, there is a vast number. In Christianity, Islam, and other religions, their actual number is known only to the Divine God. Also, when you consider that each person can have an entire team of angels, that just makes it almost impossible to know how many of them exist.

Personalities

Angels have their names. You can communicate with them in meditation to learn what their names are. They also have unique personalities, can think and communicate with one another and all of life. Contrary to some beliefs, they have free will, able to choose between good and evil. That's why a few of them chose to rebel against God and became known as the Fallen Angels.

Rankings

The angel with the most authority and power is the Archangel, Michael. After him, you have the six-winged Seraphim, who are close to the throne of God. Then there are the Cherubim, who perform special duties, such as guarding the entrance to Eden after the fall of man.

Some angels take care of "every blade of grass," feeding, caring, and providing for every plant and animal. Then there are those who, according to Islam, "write all the souls of men." These are the *kiraman katibeen,* meaning "honorable scribes." Islam says that everyone has two of those, and they note every good and bad thing you do. You can see this sentiment is echoed in cartoons and movies, with an angel on one side and the devil on the other.

The Archangels

There is some debate about the superior angels, usually because there are various factors to consider. Among these factors is the proximity of the angels to God and power. Power itself depends on various lines of thought. The Seraphim are closest to God, other than the Holy Spirit. They are celestial, the highest-ranking group in the Choirs of Heaven, and comparatively the most ethereal beings.

Archangels, however, act as the driving force of the Hosts of Heaven. Their power is beyond magnificent, and they are the ones who control Heaven's demiurgic powers as well. They interact with the physical world more than the Seraphim, and they have the power to cause changes in it. If there's any power opposed to them, they can squash it right away. The archangels are also called the Watchers, as they must look after humanity and its affairs.

The *De Coelestia Hierarchia of Pseudo-Dionysius,* written sometime during the 4th to 5th century CE, says that there are nine levels to the hierarchy of the Hosts of Heaven. In ascending order, they are:

- Angels
- Archangels
- Principalities
- Powers
- Virtues
- Dominions
- Thrones
- Cherubim
- Seraphim

In the canonical Bible used by Protestants and Catholics, and in the Islamic Quran, only two archangels are mentioned: Michael and Gabriel. The Qumranic text known as the <u>Book of Enoch</u> talks about seven of these beings. The other five have varying names inspired by Mesopotamia's Babylonian Civilization, but they're usually called Raphael, Raguel, Uriel, Zerachiel, and Remiel. These archangels played a significant role in dealing with the Fallen Angels.

The stories of the fallen ones are ancient, even older than the Bible's New Testament. However, it is believed that these stories were first gathered in 300 BCE. These stories originate from the First Temple Period of the Bronze Age, during the 10th century BCE. King Solomon's Jerusalem temple was built at that time. You can also find stories much like these in ancient Hurrian, Greek, and Hellenistic Egypt.

Archangel is a word connected with the Abrahamic religions, but you can find them across all kinds of traditions. In Islam, Christianity, and Judaism, Gabriel, and Michael feature prominently. Some Protestants insist that the only archangel there is Michael. According to the Book of Tobit, a deuterocanonical book, Raphael is considered a chief angel - a belief that Orthodox and Catholic churches also have.

In the Roman Catholic Church, angels Michael, Gabriel, and Raphael are revered with a feast. In Islam, these angels have different names: Mikal, Jibril, and Israfil. The Book of Enoch and other Jewish literature refers to an archangel called Metatron, who is known as the highest-ranking angel. However, there is no canonical acceptance of Metatron across all variations of the Jewish faith.

Archangels in Zoroastrianism

As previously mentioned, Zoroastrianism has the earliest concepts of angels. The Zoroastrians have the *Amesha Spentas,* meaning "immortal holiness." These are seven divine entities that are from the Ahura Mazda or the ultimate God. They have immortal bodies. In our world, their function is to guide, protect, and inspire us all. They do the same for all beings in the spirit world as well. In the Avesta, a compendium of Zoroastrian texts written in Avestan, we learn of the nature and origin of the Amesha Spentas or archangels.

Ahura Mazda wanted to maintain balance in all creation, so he decided to distinguish or create Spenta Mainyu, his Holy Spirit, the archangel of righteousness. Along with the Holy Spirit, he also made six extra Spenta Mainyu help form the material world as we know it. He was in charge of creating 16 lands, each with their special cultural catalysts that led to very distinct groups of humans. The Amesha Spentas were then given the task of protecting these lands and helping the humans connect to God in service. These are the Amesha Spentas, as attributes of Ahura Mazda:

- Spenta Mainyu, meaning "Bountiful Spirit."

- Ameretat, meaning "Immortality."

- Asha Vahishta, meaning "Highest Truth."

- Haurvatat, meaning "Health" or "Perfection."

- Vohu Mano, meaning "Righteous Mind."

- Spenta Armaiti, meaning "Holy Devotion."

- Khsathra Vairya, meaning "Desirable Dominion."

Archangels in Judaism

According to the Hebrew Bible, the term *malakhi Elohim* means "Angels of God." *Malach* is Hebrew for "angel," meaning "messenger." So, the angels of God are his messengers sent to execute various tasks and missions. They are the sons of God, the holy ones who execute God's orders.

In Jewish literature, it is not common to find angels. However, they show up in texts like the Book of Daniel. One briefly appeared in the story of Jacob as he wrestled with it. Lot received a warning from angels about the death and destruction coming to Sodom and

Gomorrah. In the Bible, the very first character to mention the name of an angel is Daniel. Therefore, it is believed that during the Babylonian captivity, the Jews became interested in the concept of angels. Rabbi Simeon ben Lakish, also known as Shim'on ben Lakish or Reish Lakish (230 to 270 AD), claimed that the Jews brought back specific angel names from Babylon.

Post-Biblical Judaism saw particular angels with unique roles, personalities, and undeniable significance. While it was believed that they were part of the heavenly host, there was never any clear hierarchy. The Kabbalist and Merkavah Jewish mysticism systems consider Metatron to be the highest of all angels. The Talmud mentioned him briefly, while the mystical texts of the Merkavah feature him prominently. Gabriel shows up in the Talmud for a brief spell, in the Book of Daniel, and an impressive number of Merkavah texts. Michael is also thought of fondly as being Israels' advocate and warrior.

The Kabbalah posits that there are 10 archangels. Each one corresponds to a sephira on the Tree of Life. They are:

- Metatron
- Sandalphon
- Jophiel (or Raziel, other times)
- Gabriel
- Tsaphkiel
- Michael
- Tzadkiel
- Haniel
- Khamael
- Raphael

Archangels in Eastern Orthodox Tradition

In this tradition, archangels number in the thousands. However, only seven of them are revered by name. Uriel is often considered a part of the venerated seven. Barachiel, Jegudiel, and Selaphiel are also named. Jeremiel is an eighth angel, sometimes considered an archangel.

Michael in Hebrew translates to "Who is like (or equal to) God?" He is a commander. In his left hand is a branch of green palm, while in his right is a spear that he attacks Satan with. On top of the spear is a ribbon made of linen with a red cross. He is the Guardian of the Orthodox Faith, combating all heresy.

Gabriel means "Might of God" or "God is my strength." He oversees God's mysteries, especially God's incarnation, and all mysteries connected to that. In his left hand is a green jasper mirror. In his right hand, he has a lantern with a taper on fire inside. The mirror represents God's wisdom as a secret mystery.

Raphael means "God heals," or "It is God who heals." In his left hand, he carries a physician's alabaster jar. With his right hand, he leads Tobit.

Uriel means "Light of God" or "God is my light." In his left hand is a flame, and in his right hand is a sword.

Sealtiel means "God's intercessor." He has his hands in prayer on his bosom and his eyes and face lowered in supplication.

Jegudiel means "God's glorifier." In his left hand, he has a three-thonged whip. In his right hand, he holds a golden wreath.

Barachiel in Hebrew translates to "Blessed by God." He has a white rose that he holds against his chest.

Jerahmeel translates to "God's exaltation." He inspired thoughts in humans that direct them toward God.

Archangels in Protestantism

In the Protestant Bible, you have three angels: Gabriel, also known as "the man Gabriel," the archangel Michael, and Apollyon, also known as Abaddon, mentioned in the book of Revelation, chapter 9 verse 11. In Protestantism, you have the Methodists and Anglicans. These two groups recognize four archangels: Michael, Gabriel, Raphael, and Uriel. However, some Anglican churches recognize seven archangels. When this is the case, they add Zadkiel, Jophiel, and Chamuel to the list.

Archangels in Occultist Traditions

Occultists connect the archangels to the elements, seasons, directions, and even colors. When it comes to ceremonial magic based on Kabbalistic beliefs, the four main archangels (Michael, Gabriel, Uriel, and Raphael) represent the four directions or quarters. Their colors are believed to have unique magical traits. Satanists and some non-Satanists consider Satan or Lucifer as an archangel too. However, the non-Satanists maintain the Christian view that Satan is an evil angel who has fallen from grace.

The Lesser Banishing Ritual of the Pentagram is a ritual of ceremonial magic. It was designed by order of the Golden Dawn and is now popular in most occult sects of today. The ritual often precedes all other magical rituals and rites. In this ritual, magicians say the words "Before me, Raphael; Behind me, Gabriel; On my right hand, Michael; On my left hand, Uriel...."

The bottom line of this entire chapter is to familiarize you with the concept of angels and help you understand that regardless of your beliefs, religion, status in life, or any other metric, angels can and do serve one and all. There is nothing to preclude you from enjoying the benefits of connecting with these divine beings. Chances are that in your professed faith, angels are accepted and will help you with whatever you need.

Chapter Three: The Archangels of the Four Directions

The four archangels are in charge of the four cardinal points, keeping all of life in balance and harmony. They are also called the "Archangels of the Four Corners," or "Four Directions," or "Four Winds."

- Michael (South)
- Uriel (North)
- Raphael (East)
- Gabriel (West)

Archangel Michael

Michael is also called Mikal, Mika'il, Beshter, Sabbathiel, and Lord Michael. He is in charge of the entire Tree of Life and oversees the 5th Ray, also known as the Blue Ray. You'll know Michael's around when you can see flashes of purple or blue light. He is in charge of the Fire element. Michael was officially canonized in 1950 as Saint Michael.

Protection

This archangel is known for offering protection for all of humanity. He is the Prince of the Archangels, the one who bears the Sword of Freedom with which he defends mankind. He is the guardian angel of the universe, responsible for ensuring order in all life – the archangel you turn to when you need help.

Since he has a protector role, it is little wonder that Michael's been dubbed the Patron Saint of Police Officers. He helps the good ones carry out their duties of protecting and serving their fellow humans. This archangel defends everything pure and is the very epitome of valor. He always helps protect our lives, loved ones, reputations, belongings, vehicles, spirits, and everything that concerns us.

Finding Truth and Sticking with It

He's the one to turn to when you seek to be more aware of life on every level. He'll help you come face-to-face with your true self and understand the real motivations behind why you act the way you do. Being the archangel of truth means he can help you figure out who you are so that you can live your life from a place of authenticity.

Sometimes in life, you need to change your direction or find a new purpose. You need to make tough choices. If you need help with this, call on Michael. He's great at helping you find true North. Michael will help you if you have trouble dedicating yourself to your goal, don't feel motivated, or are struggling to remain committed to your beliefs. If you have trouble speaking your truth, ask Michael to help you, and he will.

Courage and Fearlessness

When you need a sense of ambition, some faith in yourself, strength, honor, respect, courage, empowerment, and unconditional love, you can always call on Michael. He will satisfy you with these things in a way that works out even better than you could have imagined. He has a way of fueling you with courage and endurance, helping you stay the course with your goals and dreams. He also gives you the bravery you need to take responsibility for your life and accept that the power to craft it as you please is in your hands and always has been.

Michael has several duties, but one of the most important ones is to get rid of fear universally and individually. Negative energy can show up in the form of disempowering thoughts and beliefs, psychic attacks, trauma, drama, intimidation, and harassment. Rest assured, Michael is swift about nipping all that in the bud. It all comes down to how willing we are to allow him to work to the fullest extent possible. It is even better when we become conscious enough of him to establish a relationship. The same can be said of all angels and archangels.

Spiritual Protection

Michael is very particular about protecting us all from fear or situations and beings that would cause us to live afraid. The fact is that everything in this world that is ugly is very much driven by fear. In the absence of fear, there would be peace.

So, if you ask Michael to protect you from the low vibration of fear, he will work hard to keep you safe from that. He will establish a barrier between you and toxic people, experiences, and spirits that seek to pump you full of fear so that they can feast off your lack of peace. Here's the thing, though: He's not going to help you without your permission, so you've got to ask him to come through for you. Also, you need to pay attention to your gut.

If you start to feel uneasy about something or someone, or when you notice red flags about a situation, you shouldn't ignore it. Rather, acknowledge that you feel that way because something is off. Create some distance between yourself and whatever or whoever is causing you to feel uneasy; you should thank Michael for warning you and then detach by refusing to give in to fear. He'll help you with this for sure.

If you or someone you love suffers from constant bad dreams and is afraid to go to bed at night, Archangel Michael is the one to call on. Nightmares happen for several reasons, one of them being low vibration spirits. You can ask Michael to sever all connections between you and these beings and keep them out of your home. I remember when I'd just moved into a new apartment. At first, everything was fine until I started to feel like I was always being watched. At night, I would have the most intense nightmares. I thought it was a fluke that I had the same experience two nights in a row. By the third night, I was convinced I needed help. So, I called on Angel Michael for assistance. Right away, there was a shift in the energy. It felt like some oppressive aura had been suddenly vacuumed out of my space. I could sense that I was now on my own with nothing but Michael's protective, calming energy.

Sometimes you can be psychically attacked by people who are envious of you or mean you harm. Sometimes the attacks may come from someone who isn't even aware that their feelings are powerful enough to manifest as an attack. Psychic attacks can feel like you're being watched or show up as sudden intense pains in your body. Other times, it could be very unloving thoughts towards yourself that you pick up on. They seem like they're yours, but they aren't.

Guidance

Michael can help you with guidance to figure out your ultimate purpose in life, leading you to a career or life calling that will fulfill your soul. If you feel like you've hit a dead-end or have no idea what to do with yourself next, you can ask him for guidance. One way to do this is to think about what you need clarity on and then ask him to show you the answer in your dreams. Ask that the dreams be clear and easy to understand and that you're able to recall them when you wake up. Michael can also help you fix any tools or appliances that malfunction and cause a disruption in your workflow. Whether it is your cell phone, computer, car, or electric drill, you can seek his help, and he will help you get it fixed. You might get a hunch to flip a switch, or someone could swing by at the perfect time who can help you out.

Here are Michaels' magical and mystical traits:

Color: Sapphire blue

Crystal: Lapis lazuli

Chakra: Throat chakra

Element: Fire

Zodiac: Virgo, Scorpio, Leo, Capricorn

Archangel Gabriel

Gabriel is also called Jiburili, Gavriel, Jabrail, Gibrail, or Jibril. He's the second most prominent archangel in the Bible. He appears to Daniel in the book of Daniel from the Old Testament to help him make sense of the visions he had of the future. He also shows up in the New Testament, in the Book of Luke, during the Annunciation. He announced the birth of the savior Jesus Christ and his forerunner, John the Baptist. In the Book of Enoch, he acts as a messenger between God and creation. In Islam, he is the one who shows the prophet Muhammad the Quran. Gabriel is the angel of revelation because he's often the one carrying messages from the supreme God to one and all.

When you feel confused and seek wisdom in troubling times, call on Gabriel, and he will help you. He will clarify what direction to go, helping you feel sure of yourself enough to act on your decision. This archangel is also helpful when raising kids and making communication between you and others more effective.

Gabriel is shown in art with a horn that he blows. He is represented by a mirror, a lantern, a lily, a shield, a spear, a scepter, and an olive branch. Gabriel's color is white. He's often depicted as feminine with long flowing gowns, long hair, and even a feminine figure in Renaissance paintings. This is because he corresponds with the Divine feminine.

The truth is angels have no gender since their bodies aren't physical. Still, their energies can present as being uniquely female or male, depending on their roles. For instance, you've probably already worked out that Michael's energy is very masculine.

Caring for Children

Gabriel works along with other guides to care for children. They help with the entire process of having a child, right from the moment of conception to birth and beyond. They help with pregnancies, adoption, and raising the kids, too. If you find yourself in a situation where your toddler is particularly difficult, seek Gabriel's help. Have no idea what it is that's troubling them? Just call Archangel Gabriel. You might receive inspiration about what to do, or your child could just calm down, or someone could come along and help you.

Children and Purpose

Gabriel cares deeply about the well-being of children. This is the archangel who works with loving and responsible grownups that seek to nurture the young and give them good direction in life. If you work with kids, ask Gabriel to assist you and notice how much things improve.

Clarity

When you need clarity in your life and what to do with yourself, you can call on Gabriel. For instance, if you've been working on a business and nothing you do ever pans out, you can call on him. You might get a clear message that asks you to head out to a coffee shop or a bar. While it may not make sense, if you follow this message from Gabriel, you could very well run into someone doing the exact thing you want to do but succeeding at it. They could tell you what you're doing wrong, and you could implement that advice. Or you might be answered with a new idea as you wait in line for your coffee, thanks to some conversation you overhear or something.

The Divine Messenger Helping Other Messengers

People like writers, teachers, artists, counselors, and actors are messengers. If you're one of these, call on Gabriel. He will help you hone your skills and present you with many opportunities to perform in the best capacity possible. If you drag your feet rather than follow his gentle nudges, he's more than happy to give you a firmer yet loving push.

If you need help in your career, call on Gabriel to assist you. He will give you the motivation you need to finish that book, start that art piece, master your lines, and so on. If you're a writer feeling blocked, Gabriel can assist you if you call on him. Before you write or create anything, call on Gabriel and ask him to work with you, and you will find the ideas pouring through easily. You might become so lost in the creation process that you don't realize you've been in the same spot for hours on end.

Gabriel works very hard and is tenacious in all he does. Calling on him means he will inspire the same drive and tenacity in you when it comes to working. So, if you feel stuck in a rut or like you could be doing a lot better than you currently are, waste no time seeking him out.

Colors: White, indigo, orange.

Crystal: Clear quartz

Chakra: Sacral chakra

Element: Water

Zodiac: Scorpio, Pisces, Aquarius

Archangel Raphael

Raphael's other names are Labbiel, Israfel, or Azarias. He is the angel of healing. Raphel comes from *Rophe,* the Hebrew word that means "Medicine doctor." He's not mentioned in the canonical Bible (not by name, anyway). However, it is believed he's the one who would "disturb the waters" at Bethesda Pond so that people could get in and be healed. It is also believed that he's one of three angels who appeared to Sarah and Abraham to help conceive their child. Raphel is also credited with healing Jacob's injuries from wrestling and giving King Solomon his powerful ring.

According to Catholicism, he is called Saint Raphael, the patron saint of travelers, physicians, and matchmakers. In the noncanonical Book of Tobit (or Book of Tobias), he is mentioned by name. The Book of Tobit had been lost for a while. Recently, it was found in 1952 among the Qumranic Dead Sea Scrolls in a temple from the epoch of the ancient Essenes.

The book talks about Tobit, who was a helpful man devoted to the Jewish faith. He went blind and, as a result, lost all hope for life. He begged God to end his suffering by letting him die. The evening he made that prayer, a woman called Sarah also asked for the same relief from God: The relief that only comes with eternal sleep. She had lost seven husbands, and each one had passed away on her wedding night. In response, God sent Raphael. He didn't announce himself as an angel but chose the human form instead. He offered his guidance and protection to Tobias as he journied to get back the money he was owed.

Raphael then led Tobias to — you guessed it — Sarah. The two became enamored with one another and got married. Working with fish, Raphael helped Tobias eliminate the evil spirits that had murdered Sarah's past husbands. Then, still using fish, he healed Tobias' father of blindness. Together, Tobias, Sarah, and Tobit found joy in their new life. Raphael also helped Tobit get his money back. Only when he was done with all these tasks did the archangel reveal his true identity and head back to the world of angels.

The Book of Enoch refers to Raphael as one of God's holy angels who oversees human spirits. He is given the task of healing the Earth after being ruined by the Fallen Ones and their Nephilim children. He was also charged with binding a demon and casting it out, saving all children, and ridding the world of corruption. To this day, he is still doing this.

Islamic scripture refers to him as Israfel, the one who is meant to blow a large horn on Judgment Day twice to signal the end of the world. According to legend, his name was originally Labbiel. When he took God's side on creating humans, God changed his name to Raphael as a reward.

Raphael the Spiritual Doctor

Disclaimer: If you have a medical condition, please seek your doctor or another licensed medical practitioner. You can work with angel Raphael to supplement what your doctor tells you to do.

Raphael gives us access to the healing power of God. When you're dealing with some condition, you can ask him to help you, and you'll experience immediate healing. All he needs is your permission to get to work. When Raphael works to heal you, you might see a bright green aura. This aura belongs to him. It is the same one as your heart chakra. This aura shows you that Raphael is filling you with divine, loving, healing energy. You may notice this as a vision or in your dream state. You may also feel some energy buzzing around your body gently. When you're feeling out of sorts, you can say a prayer to Raphael to refresh and heal you as you sleep and then take a nap. You'll likely wake up feeling 110 percent better.

Other times, Raphael will work through a physician or other healer, especially if that's something you're more comfortable with. Suppose you've been having zero luck with doctors in fixing or figuring out your condition and how to make it better. In that case, you could call on Raphael, and he will lead you to the right medical team or healers to help you.

I remember when I was having trouble with gastroparesis a few years ago. I was sick and tired of dealing with constant nausea, the feeling of food just sitting in my gut, and the feeling of being full yet hungry all the time. I didn't want a tube in me, but I also wanted relief. After weeks of agony, it hit me: Duh! Raphael! So, I said a prayer that night before I went to bed, asking him to help me with the problem. I had a peculiar dream where there was an emerald, green waterfall. It was so beautiful, and I felt drawn to it. I bathed in it, played in it too. When I woke up, I was shocked and confused because it felt so real that my room looked like a foreign place to me for a few moments. After that dream, I could eat and drink whatever I wanted, whenever I wanted. I never again had that feeling like there was food stuck in me, sitting in my throat, waiting for me to puke! My digestion is top-notch now, and I credit that to Raphael.

Managing Pain

If you have chronic pain and inflammation, Raphael can help you, but only if you ask. Asking angels to work on something for you is permitting them to do so. When you don't ask, they can't do anything. They respect your autonomy that way. If you're managing pain after surgery or about to go in for your dental appointment, you can ask Raphel to be there with you and help you with the pain.

Travel Assistance

Raphael is the one you call on when you travel. He makes sure your trip is safe and smooth. When there's turbulence on a plane, you're stuck in traffic or dealing with some mix-up with your tickets, room bookings, or luggage, Raphael can help you smooth things out.

Comforting

There are times in life when we're beset with health issues that just won't go away. Is it your destiny to suffer this? Is this karma? Has your soul chosen this illness to teach you something? It is not clear why, but some people don't get the healing they seek no matter the routes they take to get it. In this case, Raphael can help make sure that they're comfortable by reducing the pain and discomfort and helping you remain in good spirits.

Healing Your Pets

Raphael also offers his healing energy to animals, healing all illnesses and injuries in every creature. Something about animals being more in tune with the spirit world than we are makes it easier and quicker for Raphael's healing effects to take place. Your pet will recover rapidly when you call on Raphel. Note that you can also call him to heal someone else to the extent that they are open to his energy, and he will.

Offering Guide to Healers

Being the patron saint of physicians, Raphael can help healers of all kinds. Raphael offers his knowledge and healing energy, whether in Western medicine, Eastern medicine, or African traditional medicine. If you're drawn to heal in any way, you can call on him to direct you to the best field where you can help people the most and enjoy doing so. Keep your eyes open for any signs, and listen to your gut after you pray to him for this. He can also help you out with picking the right place to study your craft and getting the money you'll need to enroll. He doesn't just stop there; he'll show you the best place to practice what you've learned. As you work to heal and comfort others, call on him. He will fill you with ideas, feelings, and visions that will lend themselves towards better results in your patients and your work in general.

Raphael's mystical and magical traits are:

Colors: Dark pink, emerald, green, green.

Crystal: Amethyst, rose quartz

Chakra: Heart chakra

Element: Air

Zodiac: Sagittarius, Leo, Aries

Archangel Uriel

Uriel's name is also Auriel, Phanuel, or Aretziel. While he's part of the four main archangels, he's one of the most mysterious ones. His traits and roles are not as clearly defined as Michael, Gabriel, and Raphael.

According to the Book of Enoch, Uriel was part of the archangels who protected the Earth from the Fallen Angels and Nephilim. In 745, Pope Zachary revoked Uriel's sainthood. He only wanted angels who were mentioned in the canonical scriptures. Despite this, the

Anglicans chose to carry on venerating him. Uriel is the patron saint of the Sacrament of Confirmation.

In Christian theology, John the Baptist was rescued by Uriel from the "massacre of the innocents" during King Herod's time. As they left Egypt, he guided John and his mother, Elizabeth, to safety. In drawings, he is shown as a cherub. It is said that compared to the other angels, he's short and chubby.

The Archangel of the Intellect

This angel gives you ideas, information, insights, and epiphanies. He is the one to call on when you need answers, innovative solutions, and creative ideas. Are you studying, writing, taking an exam? Call on him for help, and he will give you the perfect answer every time. It feels like you're getting a download of a block of thought in your mind.

All you must do is pay attention to where your thoughts go after you pray to him. If you want to make the relationship between you even deeper, just trust that the answers you're getting from him are accurate. This way, you can get clearer and more awesome answers every time. If you want to be more tactful or know the right words to set people at ease or make them more cooperative, he can help you with that. Uriel has been charged with dispensing the infinite wisdom of Divinity to humanity so that we can all express our intellectual prowess the way we're supposed to.

Uriel is also the one to call during avalanches, volcanic eruptions, earthquakes, floods, and other natural disasters, as he is the archangel of salvation. He's the one in charge of healing the planet in times like this. Tranquility and peace are his forte as well, so if you feel restless, irritated, or angry, he can help you if you call on him. Are you going through a conflict that has proven difficult to resolve or dealing with someone who isn't a fan of peace? Uriel can smooth things out either by getting them to be more agreeable or getting rid of them — not mafia-style, of course. He just sets things up so you no longer have to deal with them and move forward with your life.

This archangel is all about devotion, service, receiving, and giving. If you have trouble being a giver or receiver, he can help you realize that both ends of the stick are essential. He can help you open up to being both a receiver and a giver. If we were all that way in the world, abundance would reign supreme on Earth.

Uriel can help with illumination, light creative activities, crafts, geology, puzzles, protection from fire and flood, safety on the sea, earth sciences and geophysics, advertising and marketing, literacy and writing, and space sciences and games (like dominoes and chess).

Here are the magical and mystical traits of Uriel:

Colors: Gold, purple, and ruby red

Crystals: Obsidian

Chakra: The root chakra. Some texts connect him to the solar plexus as well.

Element: Earth

Zodiac: Libra, Gemini, Aquarius

Chapter Four: Meeting Your Guardian Angel

Guardian angels are your personal angels. They were assigned to you, even before birth, and are yours exclusively. Guardian angels are like the spiritual version of your mother in that they do everything they can to nurture you and keep you safe. They are keenly interested in your life, so they follow your journey every step of the way. They love you utterly, completely, and unconditionally and want nothing more than the best for you.

Facts about Guardian Angels

Your guardian angel can give you guidance, comfort, and support when you need it. If you're feeling lost, something hurts, or you're in a position where no one's got your back, you can trust that your guardian angels will be there for you. They will meet your needs in ways that no one else possibly could.

They can bring you great opportunities. They work to put you in touch with the right people you need to help you accomplish your goals.

Angels don't belong to any denomination. You could be Buddhist, Christian, Pagan, Jewish, and it wouldn't matter. You could identify as spiritual and still have them. The angels don't care much which religion you follow or what your culture or tradition is. All they care about is that you respect the golden rule of treating others as you would have them treat you.

Atheists also have guardian angels, despite their lack of belief in spiritual matters. The thing is, all humans have free will, and the angels would never disrespect that. They don't cross our boundaries and always honor our choices. As long as your actions and beliefs aren't deliberately hurting anyone else or yourself, they will still be there for you when you decide to call on them.

They know you in a way no one else possibly could. They know your weaknesses and strengths, your hopes and dreams, failures, and successes. They know the best path for you to follow to reach self-actualization, and they know when you're off course. They know what you need even before you're aware you need it. They know the best ways to reach out to you so you can get their message. While you might find it troubling that they know everything you've ever done, you don't have to worry about this because they would never judge you, and they love you even at your lowest low. Their love for you is unconditional to the end.

How to Reach Out to Your Guardian Angels

Learn about them. You can read books, articles, and about other people's experiences with them. There are lots of books you can find online and in a good old-fashioned library. You can also talk to your religious leader to find out what they know about angels. Hop on online forums where they discuss them, and you'll learn a lot about them.

Get ready to meet them. The first thing you have to do is *intend* to meet your angels. Simply stating that fact aloud will do. When you do, watch for signs, symbols, and names that come up a lot. Notice your dreams as well. You can set up an altar that you dedicate to connecting with your angels and meditate there at least once a day. You can also connect with them through prayer and set a fixed time each day when you'll reach out to them. Devote this time, and they will make their presence known. You can also contact them when you need help. You don't have to be in trouble before you reach out, though. It is not that they'll be mad at you for only reaching out when you need stuff, but it is nice to stay in touch anyway. You don't want to be that one friend that only ever calls when they need something, do you?

Connect with them all through your day. One way to do this is to notice the feelings you get in your gut. Pay attention to your intuition; this is one of the ways that the angels connect with us. If you don't have time to sit in meditation and you're in a tough spot, you can reach out to your guardian angel mentally and then pay attention to the message that comes to you. It helps to have a notebook where you write everything that comes to you during your meditations. This way, you can look back on what you get and implement their advice in your life. Remember that they are always with you, protecting you, caring for you. Imagine that when you must make a tough call, they're right behind you, giving you all the love and support you need.

Meditate. Before you meditate, you need to find a quiet space. Turn off all electronics and anything else that could distract you. You could turn out the lights or draw the curtains if you like. While not necessary, lighting a candle will help you keep your focus on the moment. If you have an altar, you can put it there. If you have prayer beads and would like to use that instead, you could. To set the mood, you could play some soft music with no lyrics or listen to sounds of nature like waterfalls or a fire or something.

Sit in a comfy position or lie down if you're sure you'll stay awake. Shut your eyes, breathe deeply to clear your mind. Just continue to breathe, in through your nose and out through your slightly parted lips. Just focus on your breath. When you get distracted, be glad you noticed and turn your attention back to your breath. You'll get distracted a bunch of times. It is natural, so never beat yourself up for it.

When you feel at ease and your mind is clear, you can say hi to your guardian angels. Thank them for always being with you, supporting and guiding you. If you've got a special prayer, you can recite it in your mind or out loud, dwelling on the meaning of each word.

Pay attention to what your angels tell you. You'll get subtle signs at first. It could be a fleeting picture in your mind's eye, or a warm sensation, or the feeling that you're not alone in the room. Your head might begin to sway a bit, and if you give in to that, it can become quite intense (in a good way). Come out of your meditation when you feel like it. Take your time doing so. Sit there for a moment; then you can open your eyes. Make sure you make this a constant practice by showing up at the same time each day.

Signs Your Guardian Angels Are around You

You get a sense of warmth and peace within you. This is one of the very first signs that they are near. You could be in the middle of the most troubling situation you've ever faced, and when you call on them, you feel "the peace that passes all understanding." In other words, you have absolutely no reason to feel so at ease, but you do. That's because your guardian angels are present and working on relaxing you. You can also feel a loving warmth wash over your entire body. This happens because they're around, and your heart chakra is opening as well. It has no choice but to do so once you begin to consciously connect with divinity. It is also a sign that you're more open to perceiving the insight that your guardian angel has to offer you.

You notice flashes or sparkles of light. You might notice this when your eyes are open, in which case you would notice the sparkles with your peripheral vision. Your peripheral vision is great for looking beyond the veil that hides the spiritual realm from the physical one. If your eyes are closed in meditation and turned upwards towards your third eye chakra, you might notice a golden light. The golden light signifies that you are connected to the angelic realm, and your angels are around.

You feel a warm light blanketing you. Sometimes, you might notice a warm light that surrounds you. You could even feel this warm light around your shoulders when you need some comfort. The light could also cause you to tingle all over.

You get unmistakable nudges or messages from your intuition. These nudges will encourage you when you need them, lead to positive changes in your life, and inspire you to get up and go after what you want in life. Your guardian angels talk to you through the language of intuition. You get that feeling of certainty when you have no objective reason to be so sure about something.

Your guardian angels will reach out and connect with you in subtle ways. Sometimes they're so subtle that you assume you're only listening to your internal voice, but it is really them speaking with you. When your conscious mind isn't comfortable with the idea of direct communication with your guardian angels, they'll reach out to you through your dreams or your subconscious mind. The messages you get from your guardian angels are helpful, supportive, and empowering.

Your sense of perception is enhanced. When angels connect with you, you'll notice an increased sense of awareness. You'll be hyper-aware of your environment and the energies around you. Being touched by your guardian angels inevitably causes you to be more grounded at the moment. You feel and sense everything deeply. Choosing to become aware of your environment on your own can also encourage clearer communication between you and your divine guides. Notice the air around you, the smells, the taste in your mouth, everything you can see and hear. Really sink into the feelings, noticing all of them in a relaxed way. Be in the moment, not judging anything, just observing. This is how you'll be more open to the intuitive nudges your angels give you.

You notice more and more synchronicity. When you start getting synchronistic symbols and signs that hold meaning to you, it means your angels are around. The signs tend to bring all your thoughts to a complete stop and fully ground you at the moment. You could talk to someone else about it. Still, they would likely not get it because the symbols that hold meaning for you won't necessarily apply to everyone else.

Among these synchronistic signs are angel numbers. These are repetitive numbers that you see all the time, like 1111, 222, 777, or any sequence of numbers that often grabs your attention. Other signs are finding feathers, pennies, other coins, and so on. If you find things you value, like crystals, special stones, butterflies, or anything else that causes you to pause and feel good, it means your angels are around you.

I've Noticed My Angels...Now What?

Regardless of the sign, you get that your angels are present; you can use that sign to you pause and be in the moment. Pay attention to what's happening around you at that time. There's something they want you to notice, and it may be in your environment or a particular thought you just had. Take the time to notice what it is they want you to focus on.

It might not feel easy trying to decipher what your angels are trying to tell you. Still, you will get better at this by constantly remaining aware and practicing aligning your energy to theirs. You'll be able to access their wisdom, healing, guidance, and support whenever you want.

You can ask your angels for help with deciphering your messages. Sit in a comfortable position, shut your eyes, and breathe deeply until you're relaxed. Keep your awareness and attention while remaining at ease. When you feel that stillness within you, you can reach out to your angels in your mind by making clear your intention to understand them better. Do this often, and you'll get results.

Chapter Five: Angels and Astrology

Various astrological systems and religious texts have angels and archangels assigned to the days of the week, planets, and zodiac signs. So, keep this in mind as you read this chapter. Simply work with the information here as a guideline for understanding your angels. When you meditate to connect with your personal angels, you might learn different information, so don't get too hung up on the different names. Allow your intuition to guide you, so you go with the archangels that you're drawn to the most.

The Seven Archangels of the Week

According to the ancient system of practicing magic, known as the Magic of the Angels of Men or the Pauline Art, these are the seven archangels and their corresponding planets and days.

- *Michael* — The Sun and Sundays.

- *Gabriel* — The Moon and Mondays.

- *Samael* — Mars and Tuesdays.

- *Raphael* — Mercury and Wednesdays.

- *Sachiel* — Jupiter and Thursdays.

- *Anael* — Venus and Fridays.

- *Cassiel* — Saturn and Saturdays.

Angels and Zodiac Signs

Some angels and archangels are in charge of zodiac signs. When we return to earth for another incarnation, we get to choose our Zodiac sign. Our choice depends on the lessons we need for our souls to evolve. We have options and receive guidance on the best choices for us. The lessons vary from soul to soul, and certain star signs are best to learn specific lessons. Knowing the angels associated with each sign can help you understand the sign you're born under, your unique traits, pitfalls to look out for, and your purpose in life.

Aries is ruled by Archangel Samael. This angel is connected to the Golden Ray and the "solar angels." he rules Mars, Tuesday, and Aries. If you're born under the Aries sign, you're impulsive, outgoing, and have a head brimming with ideas. You're dramatic and enthusiastic, and you never run away from a challenge. Your personality is dominant, but only because you have inner feelings of insecurity and inadequacy that you'd like to keep hidden. So, you may put up a brave front all the time, but deep down inside, you feel unsure of your choices and whether they'll pan out. You don't care much for details and can be quite the hothead, although your anger doesn't last very long, and you are quick to forget your grudges.

Other systems say Aries is ruled by Ariel, the healing archangel of earth, animals, fairies, nature spirits, and all of nature itself. This angel is supposed to help you to get in touch with nature physically and metaphysically. If you want to go into agriculture, have a garden, or manifest a career connected to the environment, this angel will help you out.

Taurus is ruled by Archangel Anael. He's also in charge of Fridays and Venus. The qualities of this sign are practical and reliable. Taurus is a very grounded, earthy sign. Taurus's are very aware of material and physical comfort and appreciative of those things. They love services and goods that are of high quality, as well as beauty and luxury. Those born under this sign are drawn to anything pleasurable to the senses. If you're a Taurus, you are very aware of nature and are practical in all your ways. You're here on earth to learn the value of patience. Naturally, you love security and stability, but you need to beware of becoming trapped by materialism.

Taurus is also ruled by the archangel Chamuel. This angel brings you inner peace when you're facing trials. If you want to have peace in all you do, whether at work or in your personal life, you can call on Chamuel, and he will assist you. He's also known as "the finding angel." If you've lost something, or you're trying to find a rare item, you can ask for his help, and you'll find what you're looking for.

Gemini is ruled by Archangel Raphael. Raphael is a healing angel and can give guidance to all healers of all sorts. He is in charge of the East. If you're a Gemini, you're quite social and skilled at adapting to whatever life brings your way. Your mind is sharp and undeniably clever. It is your main tool. You desire variety above all else, which could sometimes cause your energy to be scattered, leading to nervous exhaustion. You have an unquenchable thirst for knowledge and learning, and the more you learn, the more curious you get. You love to gather information, but you're not too big on sharing what you learn with others.

Gemini is also ruled by the archangel Zadkiel. This angel is the one to turn to when you want to truly forgive yourself or others. Forgiveness requires compassion. It is about reaching out to others and your wounded self, choosing to love despite whatever might have happened. This archangel is the one to turn to when you want to move past the memories that haunt you or to rid yourself of the pain of betrayal. If you have trouble forgiving, you can ask him to help you out.

Cancer is ruled by Archangel Gabriel. Gabriel is in charge of the West. If you are a Cancer, you are sensitive and sympathetic. You have a desire to balance emotions. You love to help others, especially when it comes to their emotional growth and development. You might seem a bit passive, but you're the living definition of the saying, "Still waters run deep." You struggle with letting go of things or people you consider yours, and as such, you become tenacious and possessive. This can lead to undesirable consequences for you. Nothing matters to you more than relationships. While you desire intimacy, you don't like that it means you must be emotionally vulnerable, so you tend to be mistrustful.

You can turn to Gabriel when you sense you have something important to share but don't know the right words to use. He's also amazing at protecting your inner child and helping you with your children as well.

Leo is ruled by Archangel Michael. This is the archangel of the Blue Ray and the South. Michael helps you communicate, protects you, and inspires you to constantly seek hidden knowledge and higher truth. If you're a Leo, you're naturally open and generous. You absolutely love praise and admiration, and so you thrive in the limelight. There's nothing you won't do to get credit in private and public. Being extremely competitive, nothing makes you happier than winning. You are a unique individual who values loyalty, especially when it comes to the people you love. You're sincere, warm, protective, and affectionate. Self-assured, you know you can handle anything that is thrown your way. On the opposite end of the spectrum, you can become extravagant, arrogant, and vain. Also, you can be quite a show-off.

Leo is also ruled by the archangel Raziel, who acts as the keeper of God's secrets, divine mysteries, and ultimate knowledge of the soul. Raziel can bring you the knowledge and will guide you to your greatest destiny if you ask him. When you have recurring thoughts, dreams, or ideas that you don't quite understand, you can ask him for assistance, and he'll make it clear to you.

Virgo is ruled by Archangel Raphael. Responsible for the East, Raphael is in charge of healing. If you're a Virgo, you have an analytical and efficient mind. You are hardworking and pay a lot of attention to the fine print. You like to thoroughly go through the options available to you before you make your choice or decision. The good things about you are that you're unassuming, helpful, and dependable. The not-so-good? You can be rather indecisive, find faults often, and fuss a lot. Also, you might criticize others (even when you don't mean to), but you're even harder on yourself. You're modest, shy, and not quite willing to push yourself front and center. You'd rather work your magic behind the scenes where no one will notice you. You're industrial, methodical, and will push yourself as hard as possible to deliver perfection — something you seek but often feel like you could never completely achieve. Whatever topic or issue you're faced with, you can master all the ins and outs easily.

Virgo is also ruled by Archangel Metatron, the lesser YHVH (Yod Heh Vav Heh, the name of the supreme God). This angel is connected to the Merkabah, or Metatron's Cube. With this sacred energy tool, this angel can clear out low energies and heal you as well. Metatron helps sensitive children and people who are new to spiritual matters. You can ask him to help you get a deeper grasp on the Universe and its mysteries.

Libra is ruled by Archangel Jophiel. Jophiel's one goal is to bring beauty to your life. He beautifies your emotions and thoughts and teaches you how to care for yourself. Sometimes he's called the "feng shui angel." He can teach you how to make your office or home more harmonious. If you feel overwhelmed by emotions and thoughts, he is the one to call on to bring you clarity. If you're a Libra, you love to weigh all sides of a matter accurately before rendering impartial judgment, not swayed by sentiment or emotions. You want a balance between soul, body, spirit, and mind. You love harmony, are diplomatic, and perform your best in a balanced and stable environment. You can see all sides of an issue, but sometimes this ability makes it hard for you to come to a clear decision. You love to socialize, and you're very refined and charming. As an air sign, you love knowledge, and your intellect is unparalleled. You love languages, and communication matters deeply to you.

Scorpio is ruled by Archangels Azrael and Camael. Azrael is a shepherd angel in charge of Pluto, while Camael is in charge of Mars. If you're a Scorpio, you're intense, and your personality is powerful. Pluto is also known as the "planet of hidden things," so you are drawn to mystery and are mysterious yourself. You can become obsessed with all that's happening around you. Your emotions are deep and powerful. When you consider something or someone as yours, you will fight to the death for them because giving them up is simply not an option. However, once you decide you're done or no longer interested in someone, the disconnection from them happens in an instant. It is unmistakable. Nothing and no one can change your mind, and you can be rather ruthless when required. The good thing about you is that you're fiercely loyal and have a sense of responsibility. However, you can get insanely jealous, possessive, and destructive both externally and internally. If it even enters your head that someone has betrayed you, you will relentlessly exact revenge.

Scorpio is also ruled by Archangel Jeremiel, whose job is to lead the souls that have passed on. Jeremiel helps them go over their lives to see the lessons they've learned from that incarnation. He can also help people still on earth go over their lives so far and develop a better approach to it. If you're afraid of death, whether it is yours or that of a loved one, call on Jeremiel, and he will help you.

Sagittarius is ruled by Archangel Zadkiel. He works with Violet Ray and is all about self-transformation and growth in spirit. If you're born a Sagittarius, you are adventurous, optimistic, imaginative, and intuitive. Sometimes you're out of touch with reality. You're not a fan of restrictions at all. You have many wonderful visions and ideas but putting those to work is something you'd rather delegate. You'd make an excellent teacher or philosopher as you love to share your ideas with others. You're generous, enthusiastic, positive, creative, a lover of life, and very creative. Your not-so-great traits are you can be tactless, opinionated, dogmatic, and you absolutely hate being told what you should do.

Archangel Raguel is also in charge of this sign. He helps you out with misunderstandings and arguments. If you want to make peace with someone or live a life of harmony, you can call on him. Trust that he will help you mediate fights and solve disagreements amicably.

Capricorn is ruled by Archangel Asariel. If you're a Capricorn, you're very responsible and careful in all you do. You want to have status and a respectable position in life. Social acceptance matters to you. Being very ambitious, you don't shy away from hard work. You'll grind long and hard hours just to get to your goal. Your willpower and determination are unparalleled. Whether your goal is money, power, fame, or love, you will stop at nothing until you have what you want. You are very talented at organizing and maintaining control. You have structure in your life, and you always expect it. You're disciplined, resourceful, refusing to waste time, money, or resources. You're very big on family traditions, and it matters to you to act in a way that agrees with society. Front and center on your mind is wealth. You want to amass as much of it as you can because you love the security you get from it, bringing you to leadership and authority positions. Beware of your tendency to worry yourself too much. You can be a tad too cautious and pessimistic.

Aquarius is ruled by Archangels Cassiel and Uriel. Being an Aquarius, you're about humanitarian and idealistic matters. Uriel oversees the North, while Cassiel is considered a "shepherd angel." You're progressive and independent as an Aquarius. There's nothing you love more than being of some assistance to humanity. Ironically, you're not good with personal relationships. You may seem unsympathetic, aloof, and cold to others. However, you have enthusiasm for your courageous ideals. Sometimes, your enthusiasm can border on fanaticism. Your mind is very sharp and developed. Archangel Uriel is the angel of intellect who can help you with epiphanies and creative ideas. Pray to him if you need to decide quickly or come up with out-of-the-box ideas.

Pisces is ruled by Archangel Zadkiel. If you're a Pisces, you are very much about your feelings. You act only based on your feelings rather than logic. You are romantic, idealistic, sensitive, and self-sacrificing, especially when it comes to love. You love being in love, and you're romantic about love and everything else. Everything about your life involves love. If it doesn't, you're not interested in it. You're peace-loving, kind, and quick to console people who are sad or in pain. You look for the underdog and root hard for them. You're sympathetic, generous, and understanding, and your sensitivity can sometimes make you irritable or moody. You're imaginative, inspirational, and resourceful.

Pisces is also ruled by Archangel Sandalphon, who helps us get our messages and prayers to God. He also helps composers and musicians. When you call on him, pay attention to the songs that come up in your mind or any words that keep repeating in your head or around you, as that could be the answer you seek.

Chapter Six: How to Invoke an Angel

Angels respect your free will, so if you want them to step in and change things on your behalf, you need to invoke them. This is the process of inviting them to be with you, connect with you, give you the support, love, and healing you need.

Invoking your angels is simple. All you have to do is just say, "Angels, I need you now," and they're right there with you. A simple prayer from your heart can summon them to you. Sometimes, your angels will come to you on their own accord, but you don't have to wait for them to come to you before you can connect with them. You have nothing to fear from summoning angels as they are benevolent.

Prayers to Summon Your Angel

Invoking Archangel Michael

If you need protection, then you already know Michael is the one to call. Here's the classic prayer for summoning him:

> *"Saint Michael the Archangel, defend us in battle,*
>
> *be our protection against the wickedness and snares of the devil.*

May God rebuke him we humbly pray;

and do thou, O Prince of the Heavenly host,

by the power of God,

cast into hell Satan and all the evil spirits

who prowl about the world seeking the ruin of souls. Amen."

You may not be going into actual battle in the traditional sense. Still, you can think of the many times you've had to battle with a toxic person, a backstabbing friend, or a lying coworker. Michael can help you out if you reach out to him with this prayer.

If you find yourself in a dark place emotionally, call on Michael. Whether it is because you've lost a family member or a dear friend, you can call on him, and he will help you. Here's another good prayer:

"Archangel Michael, I request your protection here and now.

Archangel Michael, grant me strength that I may be strong

for those around me.

I summon the strong warrior angel that I may

keep those I love from harm and pain."

If you'd rather use a more conversational prayer, you can do that. In fact, it might be better for you, as you can make the prayer more meaningful and personal.

Invoking Archangel Gabriel

You can invoke Gabriel when you're having trouble communicating effectively or at all. Here's a prayer you can use:

"Archangel Gabriel, please give me your assistance

that I may express my feelings in the best way.

Archangel Gabriel, light my path

so I can see beyond pride and ego to my authentic self

and follow your guidance in this affair.

I call upon you, Archangel Gabriel, to give me the energy I need

to go beyond the world of flesh and deep into the world of spirit,

that I may connect with my Guardian Angels better than ever. Amen."

Invoking Archangel Raphael

If you need emotional, spiritual, mental, or physical healing, turn to Raphael. Also, if you feel like your spiritual practice has taken a hit, he can help you. Here's a good prayer to use to invoke him:

"Archangel Raphael, I call upon you.

I seek your power that it ease the pain I feel.

Let your healing light wash over me,

body, soul, and spirit.

That I become healthy and whole on all levels. Amen."

Prayer to Your Guardian Angel

You may share a connection with various angels, but the ones that will be most special to you are your guardian angels. They belong to you and you alone. For this reason, you will always share a deep, spiritual bond. To connect with them, you can use your own prayer that feels right to you, or you can use this popular prayer that has worked for many:

"Angel of God, my guardian dear to whom His love commits me here,

ever this day be at my side to light, and guard, to rule, and guide. Amen"

Tips for Connecting with Angels

Always be ready to feel them around you. Angels are always with you. Assume that you can reach them anytime you want. Assume that you're being looked after and watched every moment, every day. Take a moment to breathe deeply, feel their love, and thank them.

Connect with your intuition more often. There's nothing more than your angels want than for you to be able to see yourself the way they see you. For them to show you how wonderful your soul is, you need to use your intuition — the soul's language — to connect to them. You need to be in touch with your own soul first if you want to have an easier go of reaching out to your angels. So, the best way to do this is to always pay attention to what your intuition tells you about people, places, food, things you want to do, situations you're faced with, and so on. With time, your angels will find it even easier to communicate with you through your intuition.

Place your hand over your heart as you ask them for help. Putting your hand over your heart activates your heart chakra, making you more open and receptive to your angels.

Learn the language of angels. Besides your intuition, angels will speak to you using symbols, synchronicity, riddles, metaphors, and dreams. The best way to hear them is to pay attention to the silence within you. Look beyond words and focus more on the rhythm and frequency within. They can also reach out to you with flitting light, sparkles, or scents that remind you of fond times or loved ones. Pay attention to songs that get stuck in your head or a weird, seemingly nonsensical, or random message. You simply have to trust whatever you get and always follow your intuition. The more you do this, the more everything in life becomes a medium for angels to reach out to you with.

Notice the creative answers you get. You might ask them a question, and then moments later, there's a dove at your window. You might see a unique license plate that tells you what you want to know.

You might overhear a conversation that gives you an idea. You could tune into the radio just as the announcer says something significant to you. You could pick up a book perfect for your situation. Your angel might connect you to the right people or steer the conversation between you and a friend into territory that will help you. They could give you a clear idea that pops into your mind seemingly out of nowhere. You might get a phone call, find feathers close to your home, or dream of your angels. There is no limit to how they can get their message across or answer your invocation.

You can summon them by singing their names. If you want to summon the archangels, you can slowly sing their names over and over. You'll know when they show up because your body will feel it, and your mind will become at peace and still. If you know the name of your guardian angel or angels, you can sing that too, and they'll make their presence more known and felt.

Work with your imagination. Your imagination is a good way to reach out to your angels. It is very real. In fact, it is where everything physical springs from. No one object or action wasn't first imagined in someone's mind before it became a thing. You can imagine you're connecting with them and that your relationship is becoming so obvious that it is difficult to deny. You'll start to notice great results after that.

Notice the differences when it comes to angels and their frequencies. The more you pay attention to the energy or frequency around you at different times throughout your day, the better you'll get at knowing the angels. Begin by noticing your own soul. Shut your eyes and notice what comes to you. What tone, color, or vibration are you getting? When you spend time with your loved ones, what colors and feelings do they evoke in you? When your guardian angels show up, what colors come to mind? What feelings do you have, physically and emotionally? You're expanding your range of consciousness as you do this each day. It will make it easier to detect the presence of angels around you.

Be open and flexible. It is one thing to receive guidance from your angels and another thing entirely to follow through on the messages you get. You should be willing to listen and stay open, even when they're suggesting things that aren't familiar to you. Growth comes from being outside what's comfortable for you, anyway. Trust them without question or hesitation, and this will lead to wonderful interactions and experiences.

Pray to the angels to help you connect with them better. Suppose you're struggling with figuring out their messages or even believing that they are there with you. In that case, you can pray to them to make it easier for you to understand them. Ask them, "Help my unbelief." They're not going to be offended that you find it hard to accept they're real. Asking them for help with this will yield results and open you to a world of angelic wonder.

Understand that you're the player, and they're your coach. In other words, your angels could have told you over a decade ago to buy Bitcoin. Still, if you didn't act on that, you have only yourself to hold accountable. You should always act on what they tell you to do. Sure, they can influence things and people so that they line up perfectly for you, but if you don't step up to the plate, don't get mad if you don't get what you want.

Ask them what will be in your best interests. Sometimes, we think we know exactly what we want, but that's not always the case. Your angel has a bird's eye view of your life, from start to finish. That includes all the possible routes you can take to your ultimate destination, your goal, or whatever your purpose in life. It is much better to seek their wisdom and guidance rather than assume you know all there is to know about you. So, ask them to show you the way forward and be willing to do the unfamiliar.

Say hi. Really, you don't have to be in trouble or need before you can call on your angels. Angels love nothing more than to commune with you. Say hello. Say thank you for all they've done and continue to do for you. Let them know that you appreciate them deeply, and this will spur them to reach out to you more often and do even more than they already have. Acknowledge them when good things come your way or when troubling things have been resolved. Acknowledge them when they send you signs. The more you do this, the more often you will feel their presence and get their message.

Always expect that they'll help you. Expectation is a magnet. When you expect that you'll receive help or guidance from angels, you'll get it. The more you're in the habit of expecting it, the more you'll get it. Cultivate an attitude of divine nonchalance because you know that no matter what you're going through, your angels are always with you. No matter how "late" it seems, they'll always deliver right on time. That's the attitude you should have. Expect the angels to surprise and delight you, and they will.

Here's a fun story. When I was on "the struggle bus," I had taken a loan that I couldn't afford to pay back. The due date to pay it back loomed closer and closer, and I continued to tell myself that I would simply trust that I would somehow be able to take care of it. Well, the day finally arrived, and I still didn't have enough money to pay back the loan. At this point, a part of me felt delusional, but this odd peace came over me. I continued to believe that it would be sorted out. Soon, morning became evening. Still, I continued to trust.

By 6:30 PM, my phone rang. I'd made some candles once for a friend of mine, and she absolutely loved them. She said she needed me to make her some. I told her I didn't have any wax or fragrances, and she said, "Oh, no worries! I'll send you some money for those, and I'll also pay you for the candles this time, and no, don't you dare fight me on that!" She hung up right away. A few minutes later, I got a credit transaction alert. It was double what I needed to repay the loan and more than enough for me to help make her candles. I opened the loan app and sorted it out right away. Who do you think helped me out? My angels, of course!

I learned a long time ago to always expect things to be sorted out on my behalf because I have a team of angels who *always have my back.*

Chapter Seven: Angelic Signs to Look Out For

Ever found a curious-looking feather or penny as you walked down the street and wondered if there might be an angel nearby? Well, you were probably right. Sometimes they send us very subtle messages, almost easy to miss if we're not spiritually aware, through intuitive nudges and emotions. Other times they can be obvious, especially when the message is repeated in the same form and is inexplicably out of the ordinary.

Think of this section of the book as a guide, not the law. At the end of the day, no one is better than you at working out what's a sign and what isn't and what it might mean to you. We've touched on a few of the signs in previous chapters, but now we're really going to get into them.

A white feather: Think of the white feather as a calling card of sorts. It could mean an angel is nearby, especially if you find it in an unexpected place like in your home, or your purse, or similar. Usually, you won't have an explanation as to how and why a feather would show up where you found it. It is a sign from your angels, letting you know that they're close and you're looked after. It is a message of reassurance and encouragement. They could be telling you not to quit or that the thing you're striving for is almost yours. They're letting you know that they're doing their best to make sure things work out for you to your highest good.

Coins: There's a phrase that goes, "Pennies from heaven." When you find dimes or pennies or other coins in weird places, it could be your angels reaching out to you. They want you to know that they support you, and they love you. Depending on the coin, it could have a special meaning. It might have something to do with what you're going through. It could spark an answer to the question you've been trying to figure out for a while. When you find these coins, stop, and think about what you were thinking about just before you saw them. Notice the metal and year of the coin, as well as any special markings on it. Do any of these things hold meaning for you? It is just something to consider.

Flashing lights: Sometimes, you might notice the light around you doing strange things. Through your peripheral vision, you might notice some shimmering or sparkling that you can't quite explain or shafts of light that move around you. It could also be a mirror or some other reflective surface glinting brightly when there's no sunlight or other light source around that could cause that. Sometimes, you could see an orb of light. These orbs can even show up in photographs. When you notice these inexplicable lights, chances are your angel is near.

Rainbows: It is believed that rainbows on a sunny day with no rain means angels are around. The rainbow is an encouraging sign, filling the heart with hope. It reminds you that whatever you're going through, if you just hold on a little while longer, the sun will eventually shine on you, and things will work out. It is also a sign from your angels telling you to have some more faith in yourself, that you have all you need to push through and succeed.

Messages directed at you: Remember my story about the man with the shirt that read "You'll Never Walk Alone?" This is an example of a direct message from your angels. Sometimes that message could be on a billboard, in a book, or in a magazine. You'll know it is for you because you won't be able to dispute the gut feeling you get or the fact that the words are so connected to something you've been dealing with. You could be passing by a bookshelf, and one falls out in front of you, opening to a page with a message you need. These are ways your angels reach out to you.

Chills, goosebumps, and tingling: Sometimes, when angels are around, you might get goosebumps, chills, or a tingling sensation in your upper arms, the back of your neck and shoulders, or at the crown of your head. Sometimes the sensation is subtle. I get intense surges that begin from the back of my neck and radiate through to the top of my head. When that happens, I go somewhere quiet, let the angels know I'm listening, and note what they have to tell me. Other times, you might feel a warm sensation. What's happening is that the angels are raising your vibration to connect with them better and understand what they want to share with you. Other times, they simply confirm that you're on the right path with whatever you were thinking or doing just before you got that sensation. They could also be signaling you to rise in consciousness or notice what comes next.

Feeling touched: Sometimes, you might feel a light brush or touch on your neck or arm. You could also feel like you're being hugged or like someone's patting you on the back or shoulders. It feels warm and nice when they touch you like that. It is one of the most reassuring feelings ever!

Symbols in the clouds: Others may refer to it as pareidolia, but you know for a fact that the image you see in the clouds is from your angels. You could see the shape of an angel or angel wings, flowers, hearts, or any other thing that has meaning to you. Angels love sending us cloud messages as they're beautiful to look at and cause you to pause and be in the moment. They can also create these shapes in bath foam, shadows, and tea leaves at the bottom of your cup.

Scents: Notice that there's an inexplicable sweet scent in the air suddenly? Or maybe a smell that takes you back to a pleasant time? If there's no one wearing perfume, you didn't use any air freshener, and there's no reason the place should smell the way it does, then that means there's an angel around. They can smell like yummy food, perfumes, flowers, and any other pleasant smell. Sometimes you could be hanging out with a group of people, and only you and a few others notice the smell. If the smell reminds you of the scent of a loved one who has passed on, then it could be that they're right in the room with you along with your angels. When you're hit with sudden smells, think about what they remind you of, and note what you were thinking about before you noticed the scent.

Television and music: Angels can communicate with you through media platforms as well. You might be switching from station to station or channel to channel, only to land on one where certain words that apply to what you were just thinking come on, whether in a show or a song. Or you might find a movie or a show that directly ties into something that's happening to you.

Ringing ears: This is way different from tinnitus. When angels need you to pay attention or want to pass along a message to you that you may not quite be ready for at that moment, they'll let you have it in the form of a "download." This is information that will become relevant later. When you get this download, a sound accompanies it, like buzzing, or ringing bells, or a high-pitched sound in one ear that suddenly makes you hyper-aware of the moment. It could be loud or quiet. If it ever gets too loud, you can let your angels know, and they'll turn it down. Usually, it doesn't last longer than a few seconds.

Coincidences: I always say there's no such thing as coincidence. Esther Hicks, the author of Law of Attraction, refers to them as "cooperating incidences" that have been set up by your higher self or angels or Infinite Intelligence to guide you to what you seek. The next time a coincidence happens, reframe it in your mind as your angels alerting you to their presence, or a message, or giving you a sign about where to go next.

Phone calls: Have you ever thought about someone you'd meant to talk to for a while now, and then your phone rings, and they're the one calling? The reason you had that thought is because of your angels. They may have caused that person to think of you so they could help you with something you're struggling with, whether that's a connection or some words of wisdom. Other times, it could be that person was going through something, and their angels reached out to yours to let you know you should answer the phone when they call you.

Noticing intense beauty around you: You could be going through the worst things when suddenly you look around, and everywhere looks magical. You look at the sky, and it looks so beautiful it is surreal. You notice birds singing, and you pick up on a melody so good it forces you to shut your eyes and smile. These moments could be your angels doing what they can to raise you from lower vibrational thoughts to a place of joy, calm, and serenity.

Butterflies: These lovely creatures are considered gifts from the ones we've loved and lost, letting us know that they're still with us and that they are doing just fine on "the other side."

Angel numbers: These are a form of synchronicity. If you always see certain number sequences, over and over, then it could be your angels reaching out to you. You might always look at the time when it is 11:11 unconsciously. You might have gotten three receipts in a row with $11.11 or with 1111 on the transaction ID or something. Someone might say 888 randomly, or you may notice you tend to look up from your phone when a car with 333 as part of its license plate number passes by. You might notice that you always wake up at 5:15 or 4:14 in the morning. These are ways your angels reach out to you. You can find them on addresses, phone numbers, store prices, and even hear random strangers say the words. You can hear them on the radio, see them on the television, or measure something that amounts to an angel number. You can look up the meanings of these numbers online, and you'll know exactly what your angels are trying to tell you. If you would rather meditate than get a general meaning of the numbers online, you can do that. Here's a quick summary of the most common angel numbers:

• **000:** You have support from your angels as you begin new things. It also means it is time for you to begin something new.

• **111:** Your desires are in the process of being manifested. Prosperity is being drawn into your life, and the angels are there to help you with this.

• **222:** You require trust and balance. You want to find peace in your relationships and in yourself. You may also be about to start something new and harmonious in your life.

• **333:** You need to really give your creative pursuits your all. Your angels will support you and inspire you all through your creative endeavors.

• **444:** Your angels want you to look within and honestly seek answers for the troubles you face. This is the number of inner wisdom and honesty. This number also says you've been hard at work and that you will soon reap the results.

• **555:** Big changes are just around the corner. Your angels ask that you remain positive and confident as new things come your way.

• **666:** This number isn't a bad one – if it *is* an angel number. It tells you that you need to trust yourself, find balance, and restructure negative thoughts to empowering ones.

• **777:** Good fortune is coming to you. It could also mean you need to focus on spiritual fulfillment.

- **888:** Your hard work is bearing fruit. You should expect financial gain soon.

- **999:** This number signals completion or an ending. It is time to say goodbye to some part of your life, whether a friendship, business, job, or relationship that's run its course. You're not alone through this. Your guides are with you and will help you begin something fresh and new.

Your solar plexus: If you feel a knot in your stomach or butterflies, your angels could be alerting you to the fact that there's something off with where you are or who you're dealing with. They use your solar plexus to get you to become more aware of your environment and to be careful. If you get this feeling around a certain place or person, they could be telling you to stop going there. Or it might mean you should cut down on how much time you spend with the person or how much you tell them.

Robins coming to perch near you: These birds are thought of as deceased loved ones. They'll show up at the same garden or spot to let you know that they're always with you.

Babies and animals looking at something you can't see: Babies and animals are the closest to the world of spirit. They don't have the veil that keeps us, adult humans, from interacting freely with the spirit world. So, if you notice a baby smiling and looking at what seems to be nothing, it is probably an angel. If you notice your cat or dog tracking something you can't see with their eyes, then your spirit friends are in the room. When angels are around, pets and babies are excited but also at ease and happy.

The sense of not being alone: Sometimes, you get the sense that you're not alone even though there's no one else in the room. You might walk into an empty room, and your eyes are immediately drawn to a chair. You sense that there's someone there, even if you can't see them. You can feel love, safety, and warmth coming from this being.

Chapter Eight: Tuning into Angelic Protection

At every moment, you have the protection of angels available to you. You always have your guardian angels with you, but you should make a habit of asking them for help consciously. You don't need to see signs they're around to believe that they are working to protect you. All you need to do is request their protection, no matter the situation you find yourself in, and trust that they are right there with you. You can ask them out loud or in your mind. Remember that this is an act of co-creation, where you and the angels will create that protective barrier. You have to accept that they're protecting you and visualize them doing so.

It helps tremendously if you're conscious about their ability to assist you and aware that you can connect with their energy at any point in time. Understand that the concept of co-creation with your angels is very important. They'll help you, but you must help them help you as well. Let's talk about how you can do that.

Visualizing a Protective Light Shield

This is a potent way to feel the protection of your angels.

1. Ground your attention by focusing on your breath and the situation that has you concerned.

2. Ask for your angels and tell them to put up a shield of protective white energy all around you to keep you completely safe, no matter what happens. Make this request in your own words.

3. Ask the angels to follow you around and make sure that you remain safe.

4. Visualize a white divine light surrounding you in your mind's eye and see the angels around you. This way, you can connect energetically with the angels' protection.

5. You can either keep up this visualization or trust that your angels are now guarding and guiding you.

When you travel, you can use this by asking the angels to surround the vehicle and shroud it in white, protective light. If you're worried about your luggage, you can assign angels to take care of them for you too.

Everyday Protection

Sometimes you can decide whether to go somewhere. Other times, you really don't have a choice. If you feel anxious or uncomfortable, you can still use this method to keep yourself safe. Your angels will be more than eager to follow you around. If you are contemplating whether you should go somewhere, check in with your intuition. If you feel uncertain or anxious, then you can call upon the angels to help soothe your mind.

Note that the archangel Michael is the most powerful one for protection and shielding. So, if you're in sudden danger or an emergency, you can call on him to help you and calm you right away.

His colors are electric blue and gold, and he uses gold and purple light to protect and shield you.

Protection for Kids

Your kids can also use the shield of light to stay safe. If they feel anxious about anything they're going through at school, it will come in handy. So, teach it to them. You can also tell the angels to look after your kids on your behalf.

Protection against Bad Luck

Have you noticed that you've been having a run of bad luck lately? Then you can ask your angels to help you fix it. Ask them for help with cleansing your aura and raising your vibration to one where things begin to work out for you. Don't fall into the trap of assuming it is just a coincidence that things have been going wrong. Remember, there are no coincidences. So, take a moment to breathe, connect with your angels, and ask them to rid you of anything in your aura that draws bad luck to you.

Protection against Gossip, Slander, and Plots against You

If you're the talk of the town in a negative way, the angels can help you out. Some people just love to fabricate stories about others to make them look bad. There's no reason you should continue to put up with that. Ask your angels to protect you from the effects of the gossip and even go a step further to reveal their lies. Also, suppose anyone's actively plotting against you. In that case, you can be proactive by asking your angels to get out ahead of whatever they've got planned so that you come out of it unscathed.

No Shortcuts

You need to know that your consciousness is key when it comes to enlisting divine protection. The angels can do their best work when you pay attention to your intuition and understand that you're responsible for your decisions and actions. Don't think that the angels are some sort of shortcut or quick fix for problems you shouldn't have had in the first place. For instance, just because they will protect you doesn't mean you should leap off a cliff and see if they catch you. They're not a substitute for logical thinking. Sure, they lovingly protect us, but you must realize you're responsible for the choices you make.

How to Boost Your Connection with Angels

Keep your space clear. Sometimes we get so busy, and that busyness is reflected in the clutter that's all over our space. If you are only learning how to connect to your angels, this clutter can prove very distracting. So, make sure that you take some time to clean out your space. Take the trash out, put things where they should be, and make the place tidy. When you clear the physical, it is easy to clear the mind. You need a crystal-clear mind to get in touch with your angels. Refresh your space by opening the windows to let in fresh air and natural light. You can also cleanse the aura of your space with some sage. If you have lemon essential oil, you could add a few drops to some water in a spray bottle and spritz the room so that it has that clean, lemony smell. You could also light some candles if you want to really set the mood.

It begins with deliberate intent. It is possible to get to a point where you can connect with the angels effortlessly but to begin with, you should take some time to tune in to their frequency consciously. Turn off your cellphones, make sure all electronic devices are silent, make sure everyone at home knows not to bother you for about 15 minutes. Sit down, shut your eyes, and breathe in deeply. Then, intend to connect with your guardian angels in your mind.

Raise your vibration. You've cleared your space, and that has raised its vibration and yours as well. Now it is time to really raise your vibration. Angels are spiritual beings of light who vibrate at a very high frequency. You need to match their frequency to communicate with them and subsequently invoke their protection. Angels can and will help you with this if you ask. Just tell them to cleanse your vibration and raise it. Sit in a relaxed position as you breathe deeply. Visualize a divine, powerful white light surrounding you. Breathe this light in through your nose, and as you exhale through slightly parted lips, let go of all that's murky in your aura. If you like, you can play some relaxing music or work with a guided meditation. Incorporating peppermint, frankincense, and lavender essential oils will give you great results and help keep your mind clear and present.

Summon protection. Fear keeps people from truly connecting with angels. The way to fix this is to use a protection ritual to make you feel secure and safe. You can invoke the Divine shield of light to surround you, or you can call on Archangel Michael and his angels to watch over you as you connect with yours. Simply saying, "Thank you, Michael, for being here with me now and keeping me safe on every level of existence while I connect with my guardian angels."

Ask your guardian angels to connect with you. Keep breathing deeply and keep your awareness within you. You can place both hands over your heart and then say, "My angels, I request that you please come here, now, and connect with me. Help me so that I remember you are always present. Help me to grasp the wisdom, knowledge, and truth that will serve my highest good. Thank you."

Listen to them. This isn't a one-way conversation. You ask, therefore your angels answer. Whatever you do, don't try to force your will into hearing something. Just keep your awareness on your breath and expect that the angels will give you a response. If it helps, you can add, "Thank you, my angels, for giving me access to that which you want me to know at this moment." Stay open, keeping your mind quiet as you wait to receive their guidance. Recall that there are so many ways they could speak to you. Notice the emotions, sensations, and thoughts that show up within you. Trust what you get and write it down, so you remember it. Also, note that the most important messages can sometimes come not through your mind but your spirit and feelings.

Seek love and light. Remember that the messages you get from your guardian angels must be high vibrational ones. This means that you should feel love and light from them, and all messages should flow from that perspective. If the messages seem fearful, don't hold on to those because they're not from your angels. It could be your ego-mind interfering with the process. Shift your attention back to your breathing. Breathe in the Divine light that surrounds you, ask your angels to help you remain focused on them, and keep your heart open. If your ego absolutely refuses to shut up, you can ask your angels for help with that.

Michael's Sigil for Protection

You can work with Michael's sigil to protect yourself. You can either print it off the internet or learn to draw it yourself. It is not difficult. All you need is a pencil, Rose Wheel, ruler, and an image of his sigil. It is useful for invoking Michael's protection at any time. You can print it out on your clothing as a design or wear it as a talisman or an amulet. You can draw it at the entrance of your home to keep it safe, too. To amplify the power of the sigil, you can pray with it. You can also keep some dark purple amethyst and sugilite with you all the time. These are Archangel Michael's crystals. Make sure that you clean the crystals often in saltwater to remove all the negative energies they've absorbed to help keep you safe.

Angelic Protection Prayer

Suppose you notice that sometimes you feel drained because you've had to deal with some people or certain situations. In that case, you should invoke your angels' protection. If you tend to pick up energy from other people, places, and so on, or find yourself out of sorts, your angels can help you stop that from happening. Here is a prayer you can use to help yourself. Start your day with it.

Archangel Michael, you are the protector angel.

You are the one I turn to now.

I ask that you surround me with white light

from the crown of my head to the soles of my feet.

I ask that you fill this white light that now surrounds me

with love, healing,

harmony and protection.

I ask that your white light keep me free of all negative energy.

I ask that this white light expands from me

into any space I'm in all the time.

I ask that the angels needed to protect me

be with me in all I do this day

and every other day of my life.

Chapter Nine: Working with Michael and Gabriel

Working with Michael

You can use a very simple prayer to get in touch with Michael and work with him. I'm about to offer you one that you can use as you begin your sessions with him. Whether you'd like to use a guided meditation with Michael or just have a chat, this prayer is a good place to start. It will help you really focus your attention on him and silence the chatter in your head. It is also easy to memorize. If you'd like to change it up and make it your own, you can also do that.

Mighty Prince, Archangel Michael

Commander and chief of the hosts of heaven

You who guard souls and vanquish all spirits that dare rebel

You the servant of the most high God

You, our glorious conductor

full of excellence and virtue beyond imagination

I turn to you in confidence

asking that you save me from all evil

and help me day after day

to live in alignment with my true path.

Amen.

Suppose you have a petition for assistance or guidance with something. In that case, you can add that to the prayer before wrapping up with the final amen. There are no limits to what he can do for you, but keep in mind that he's an archangel. So, if you have other concerns that aren't life or death, you should reach out to your guardian angels instead. Other than Michael's well-known association with motivation, courage, truth, and protection, he is also great at giving you joy, friendship, forgiveness, confidence, ambition in business and career, success, and material wealth.

Saint Michael Meditation

One of the easiest ways to begin working with Michael is using a guided meditation specifically tailored to connect you with him.

This meditation is inspired by a Tibetan Buddhist meditation that doesn't require and recordings or video. To start off, you need to go somewhere quiet where you won't be bothered. Turn off all electrical devices so that you're not distracted. Make sure you're wearing loose and comfortable clothes. You can either sit down in a comfortable position or lie down. If the place is cool, you might want to wear something warm or drape a blanket around yourself so that you aren't forced to terminate the meditation because you feel cold.

When you feel comfy, shut your eyes, and pay attention to your breath. If you've never meditated before, you might find it difficult to clear your mind. Some people have more trouble than others. In this case, meditation can induce more stress than relaxation, making it hard to keep up the practice. However, you've got to keep at it. The key is not to make it work. It is totally normal to have your mind getting distracted over and over when you first start meditating. Still, the more you practice, the better you'll get at holding your attention to your breath.

Each time you notice you've been distracted, that's actually a really good thing because it means you're becoming more aware. Simply acknowledge you've been distracted, take a moment to feel gratitude for noticing, and then return your focus to your breath. It doesn't matter if you get distracted 77 times a minute. It is always a good thing to notice it, and the more you do, the better you'll get at not being distracted. This way, your meditations with Michael will grow and deepen. The more you sit in meditation, the better you'll get at sensing his presence.

You may focus on your breath for as long as you want, or you can count 11 breaths, with a full breath including an inhale and an exhale. If you notice counting doesn't work for you, keep breathing until you feel relaxed and there's absolute stillness in your mind. As you breathe, relax each part of your body. Don't think too hard about whether you're fully relaxed or need to go deeper. Just trust that you will relax deeper.

When you feel fully relaxed, imagine that there's a white light coming from your heart's center. See it spread out completely around you, enveloping you. If you'd rather envision a blue light, this is fine too, as it is Michael's color. When you become fully aware of his light all around you, keeping you completely safe, you can then call on Michael in your mind or aloud, asking him to join you. Naturally, many want to know how to be sure he has heard you. The simple answer is you just know. There's no other way to describe it. Michael's energy is very distinct from other angels and very strong. Suppose you're not already able to sense energy. In that case, you may have a different experience, but you will find his presence is unmistakable in due time.

When you can sense his presence, thank him for being there with you. There's no need to be poetic about it if you don't want to be. He loves you anyway and will always guide and protect you because that's what he's been charged to do. Let him know that you'd like to develop a relationship with him as your guardian angel. Seek his advice on anything that's bothering you. Again, you already have your own guardian angel, so it is a good idea to seek Michael for the more important stuff. Either way, trust that as long as your desire matters to you, then it matters to him too.

The way the rest of the meditation goes is your choice. You could have a conversation with him, imagining that you're both taking a walk along a peaceful path or a beach. You could simply sit in his presence in silence and let his energy refresh, motivate, and energize you to do things that you once thought were overwhelming.

Another thing you can do is hand over your negative emotions, worries, and fears to Michael. A simple statement to that effect is all you need. When you do this, you'll notice that you no longer feel like they're eating you up as they used to. You will be inspired about the next course of action, or you'll come to accept that this is a matter that you can't control, one that Michael can help you deal with. This makes all your anxiety melt away. Whatever you choose to do with the rest of the meditation, you should express your appreciation to Michael for acknowledging your call and taking care of yourself.

Protection Ritual

Michael shows up in lots of magical systems as well. Hoodoo practitioners are well aware of his power. Many eclectic witches call on him as well. If you're a practicing magician, you can call upon Michael to protect your rituals. All you need is a blue, red, or gold novena candle. Dress that candle with Saint Michael oil, orange peels, and cloves. Then burn this candle on Michael's day (Sunday), and you will have activated a powerful protection spell. While Sunday is his day, you can still work with him on any other day if you need to. He will show up for you.

Cutting Cords with Michael's Sword

It might seem strange, but there's a meditation method where you picture yourself being an energy body with threads hanging off it. Imagine that these cords signify karma that binds you from all your incarnations past and present. The cords also represent soul ties and agreements you have made knowingly or unknowingly that do not serve you. As you meditate, you can ask Michael to help you sever these cords with his sword's blue flame. In your mind's eye, see Michael raise his sword and hack away at all the cords. Then visualize your energy body as being free from them. The more you do these sessions, the more you'll notice the effects on your life.

Working with Archangel Gabriel

To recap, Gabriel can help you with pregnancy, communication, adoption, children, clear messages, teaching, writing, acting, creating art, and more.

Prayer for Better Communication

You can work with Gabriel to help you communicate clearly. He will help you speak so you're not misunderstood or confusing anyone. Do you have to give an important speech, propose to someone you love, teach a class, give a presentation, or discuss something significant? You should call upon him to help you communicate clearly. Here's a good prayer:

>*Archangel Gabriel, Most Divine,*
>
>*I reach out to you to ask*
>
>*that you help me as I communicate with others.*
>
>*Let my words and meaning be clear as crystal.*
>
>*Let there be no room for misunderstanding between us.*

Are you giving a public presentation, speech, or workshop? You can say this prayer:

>*Archangel Gabriel,*
>
>*I need your help.*
>
>*Please guide me and help me speak clearly and confidently*

*so,   everyone   understands   and   appreciates   my
presentation/workshop/speech*

and is blessed and edified by it.

Thank you.

Assistance with Childbirth and Pregnancy

If you or someone you love is dealing with pregnancy, childbirth issues, or having difficulty with conception, then you can seek out Gabriel to help you. He can guide you on the right steps to take and help you find peace during the process. There are many testimonies of people who conceived when they finally reached out to Gabriel after trying for so long. He could also lead you to try IVF or something else. Just trust that you will get an answer from him. Say this prayer:

> *Archangel Gabriel,*
>
> *My husband/wife and I desire to conceive*
>
> *a healthy, lovely child to call our own.*
>
> *Please help us. Please give us this precious miracle.*
>
> *Show us where we need to go and what we need to do*
>
> *to make our dream come true. Thank you.*

Adoption

Suppose it so happens that it is not in the cards for you to have biological kids of your own. In that case, Archangel Gabriel can assist you with the process of adopting a child. He can help you find a child who's a great fit for you and sort out any legal issues that may come up in the process. Say the following prayer:

> *Archangel Gabriel, Most Divine and merciful,*
>
> *It is our desire as a couple to find a child*
>
> *who will be as happy having us as parents*
>
> *as we would be to have them.*
>
> *We seek the child that's meant for us*

by divine will. Please help us.

Connect us with the right people and agency.

Cause your favor to shine upon us that we may be approved.

Bless the process that all rough roads be made smooth and easy.

Thank you.

Receiving Guidance

Suppose you feel confused and lost, and you can't find a way out of a situation. In that case, you can ask for Gabriel's help and guidance, and he will give you the information you need either through a dream or through someone else who has the answers. He also has direct contact with Divine Guidance, and so you can take advantage of this when you meditate with him or pray to him. Say this prayer:

Archangel Gabriel,

Please help me to easily get in touch with the Divine

so I may receive guidance that is perfect for me

with ease. This or better. Thank you.

Meditating with Gabriel

Sit in a quiet place, wearing comfortable clothes. Make sure you have no distractions around you. Shut your eyes and focus on your breath so that you can remain grounded at the moment. When your mind feels calm and still, you can call out to Gabriel or invoke him in your mind. Invite him to be with you. You'll know he's with you because there'll be a change in the energy around you. You might also notice that there's some golden copper or white light around you. This means that angel Gabriel is very close to you. When you feel his presence, you can just sit there and bask in it, or you can let him know if you need help with something that matters deeply to you. Wrap up the session by thanking him for helping you with what you need.

Chapter Ten: Working with Raphael and Uriel

Working with Archangel Raphael

When you need healing or help with any health issue, call on Raphael. He will find a way to help you, whether that's through divine intervention or by guiding you to wherever you need to go to get the treatment you seek. Raphael knows the best way to heal you with your condition. When asking for Raphael's help, you can do so either in your mind or out loud. He must have your permission before he can help you.

It helps to really open your heart to Him and pour out your feelings. Don't try to be organized about how you phrase what you feel. The chances are that when dealing with health issues, you'll feel so frustrated and tired that you can't find it in you to rein in your emotions. Lay it all on him, and don't hold back at all.

Visualizing Healing Light

Raphael's color is an emerald-green which can heal you. Lie down in a quiet place where you won't be disturbed. Make sure you're wearing comfortable clothing and that you have a blanket to keep you warm as you meditate. Close your eyes and focus on your breath. Breathe in through your nose and exhale through slightly parted lips. It is fine if the exhale is longer than the inhale. You can just keep going until you feel very relaxed yet aware.

Now, call upon Archangel Raphael in your mind or out loud. You can call his name repeatedly and feel the way the energy around you changes. As you do this, you should imagine that you're being surrounded by emerald-green light, moving in and through you.

You might notice a tingling sensation, feel some warmth, see greenish flashes behind your eyelids, or notice emerald, green flashes in your peripheral vision. When you feel he is present, go ahead and let him know how you feel and what you want help with. If you feel like crying, let it out. He will comfort you. When you feel you've completely laid it all out there, you can thank him and trust that he's going to answer you.

Ideally, you shouldn't try to dictate how you want Raphael to heal you. Just trust that he's going to do it in the best way for you. If you try to dictate how you should be healed, you might be impeding or slowing down your healing process. Allow him to work the way he wants to.

Dealing with Addiction

If you're dealing with addiction, know that you can get help from Raphael. You don't have to go through it on your own. You can work with the Divine power of Raphael to break free of the chains that hold you back.

Addictions vary in severity and can cover many things like sugar, drama, sex, drugs, the internet, shopping, emotions, working, cellphones, etc. Regardless of what you're addicted to, the underlying mechanism driving it is the desire to numb the pain from unresolved past trauma or physical or emotional pain. It is all about trying to escape from stress. The late, great Eckhart Tolle put it this way: "Addictions begin and end with pain."

We often develop addictions because we don't really know how to deal with the pain we feel. The thing about addictions is that it is not just about quitting them. It is about getting right to the heart of the matter, to the pain that leads us to seek comfort in our vices, to begin with. We need to completely heal this pain rather than numb it with substances or harmful behavior. Having been through addiction myself, I know what it is like to criticize, judge, and loathe yourself because you can't seem to stop this thing you know is bad for you. However, I can tell you firsthand that self-loathing does nothing to fix the problem. In fact, it only makes it harder to deal with. A better course of action would be to seek Raphael's help with acknowledging what's really the cause of the addiction and what role the addiction has played in your life.

Dissolving Addiction with Raphael's Help

Raphael's name literally means "God heals." This angel carries the very healing power of God, and he can help you out by addressing the pain that feeds the addiction. Other than divine intervention, one of the ways he can help you with this is to guide you to people and resources that will help you heal in truth, not just stop the habit you've chosen to fix the pain. He could hook you up with an alternative form of therapy, the right people for you, energy healing resources, and so much more. He could also help you by showing you a dream that allows you to pinpoint the root of your hurt so that you can deal with it and heal.

I used to struggle with addiction to marijuana. Some people argue that it can't be addictive. Still, as great as the plant is for medicinal purposes, experience has shown me that it absolutely can be addictive. At first, I used it to help me through some pain from surgery. Then I made a habit of having it at least three times weekly. Over the next two years (after the first time I tried it), I found that I had to start my day with it. If I had to work, I had to have it first. Heading out? About to eat? Going to bed? Have some more! It became glaringly obvious that I had a problem. Did I want to quit? Definitely, however, I would last about a day or two before going back to the habit even heavier.

Tired, it occurred to me that I needed help. So, one night, in tears, I called on Archangel Raphael. I let him know how badly I wanted to quit, how it affected my body, mind, and spirit, and how weak I felt. I wanted so badly for it to end. I asked him to help me. Then I went right to bed. In my dream that night, I saw myself as a child. I saw a relative hitting that child version of me, over and over, violently.

Before I could get to them to stop, they had taken off, leaving my little self on the floor, crying. My younger self held a doll in one hand; its head was nowhere to be found. I reached out to her, picked her up, and held her against me. As I did, I felt waves of love, release, joy, and healing wash over me. Tears fell from my eyes, but they were tears of joy. I put it down and noticed that her doll had its head back on. She looked up at me and smiled at me sweetly as she said, "Thank you."

I woke up that morning, and like every other morning before that, my hand reached for the stash that I keep right by my bed. This time though, it was different. I tried to open the box where I kept all my "paraphernalia." I just couldn't. I didn't want to anymore. I felt no repulsion or disgust but no desire for it either. So, I took the box and trashed it outside my home. That was the end of it. I have never had a craving since. After many failed attempts to quit, I didn't get the withdrawals I used to have for the first time.

I'm sharing this story with you because I want you to know that it is possible to deal with addiction and end the pain that causes it once and for all. I'm not suggesting that you shouldn't get professional help. Please, you absolutely should. I am saying that things can work out even faster if you ask Raphael to heal you.

Working with Uriel

When you choose to work with archangel Uriel, it is like having a divine mentor with you around the clock. It is great to know that he's always keeping your path lit, telling you where to go and how to be a more confident person. Uriel can help you with self-respect and self-esteem. You'll know he's around when you notice thunder, bulbs that flicker on and off, or appliances acting weird.

Praying for Knowledge and Wisdom

You can work with Uriel to learn about any situation or topic. If you're a student, seek his help with exams. Here's a prayer you can use:

> *Archangel Uriel,*
>
> *Please help me with this exam.*
>
> *I ask that you show me what I need to learn.*
>
> *Open my mind that I understand all I read and hear.*
>
> *Guide me to the right information.*
>
> *Bless my mind that I have a retentive memory.*
>
> *See me through this exam, that I give the right answers*
>
> *clearly and efficiently.*
>
> *Amen.*

You can modify the prayer to suit whatever you need help with. It could be a project you are working on, a proposal, or whatever else you need to succeed in. Uriel will grant you clear insight. If you're a student or a teacher, or you work in a field that requires you to have a lot of knowledge, you can pray:

> *Archangel Uriel,*
>
> *Please give me information that is crystal clear.*
>
> *Grant me great insight about this topic,*
>
> *and bless me with wonderful, original ideas.*

Thank you.

Prayer for Manifestation and Personal Power

You can say this prayer to Uriel if you want to manifest something or increase your personal power:

Archangel Uriel,

You light up the universe.

I ask that you shine this light of yours upon me.

Let your light illuminate my path.

Let it show me the way to the dreams I seek to realize.

Show me the way to what I want.

Make the path I should take very clear to me.

Please set me free from the chains of limitation

insight, thoughts, beliefs, and emotions.

Show me and set me free from everything

that keeps me from what is mine by Divine right.

Let your light change me for the better

and help me transmute bad into good.

Light up the shadows from my past

that haunt me still until this day.

Let your light banish them away.

Let me know and experience true peace in my heart.

I declare that I am ready to step into your light.

I am ready to tap into Universal Consciousness.

I trust that in the light of this consciousness.

I will come to deeply understand that everything happens for a reason.

With this knowledge, I find peace within me.

I choose to walk with you, Uriel.

Help me know my worth.

Help me know truly that I'm responsible for creating my life.

Reveal to me the divinity I carry within.

Show me that I have the very same power

that crafted heaven and earth within me.

Amen, and thank you.

The more you say this prayer, the more you'll come to realize just how powerful you are. You'll come to know your worth and that you deserve to have your dreams and goals fulfilled. Many people don't achieve their desires because they are unaware of how powerful they are and refuse to accept that they are worthy.

People always want to justify why they should get what they want. If someone gets a lot of money for very little work or effort, they're made to feel guilty because they didn't put in too much effort. If someone walks away from an accident unscathed, they're made to feel guilty for getting away without a scratch. It is a tough concept for many to accept that your existence is more than enough justification.

Now, it is easy to swing this argument into psycho-Ville, so to be clear, I'm not talking about horrible desires like wanting to hurt someone. I'm talking about the desires that are in alignment with your Divine life purpose. Most people don't manifest what they want because of a lack of self-worth and awareness of their power. Therefore, this is the perfect prayer to help you with that.

Connecting With Uriel

When you want to invoke Uriel, a powerful being, you want to clear your mind of negative emotions and thoughts. This way, you will find it easier to connect to his higher, purer energy. Keep your heart open, your mind calm, and he'll reach out to you. If you want to clear your mind, it helps to have a sacred space or altar to work with Uriel.

On your angelic altar, you should only have spiritual items, texts, and images that you hold sacred. To work with Uriel, it helps to have ruby red items like crystals. Spiritual items of that color represent Uriel's energy.

Sit and quiet your mind at your altar by focusing on your breath, chanting, or reciting a prayer or litany. When you find your mind is focused and quiet, you can imagine seeing Uriel with his ruby ray, or you could use this traditional invocation:

Archangel Uriel,

You are the angel of illumination and wisdom.

I am thankful to God for generously giving you his wisdom.

I ask that you please bless me with this same wisdom

and help shine God's light upon my heart.

When I am faced with life-changing choices,

Please fill me with the Wisdom of God.

Help me, that I may find innovative answers

that will give me peace of mind

and peace all my life.

Uriel is an absolute pro at transmuting negative energy into positive. To get his assistance with this, understand that spiritual lessons are to be learned from your emotions. Take the time to mine that emotion for the gems within it, and then release it.

Chapter Eleven: Working with Ariel and Azrael

Working with Archangel Ariel

Ariel is also known as the Lioness of God. She oversees all things in nature. This angel can help you to draw on the healing power of nature when you're going through difficulties. She's connected to prosperity, material needs, and manifestation powers on account of her association with the element of earth. When she's around, you will either hear the wind or see a lion in your visions.

Environmental Healing

You can work with Ariel to heal the earth of pollution, nature, forest fires, global warming, and more. Call on her to heal and cleanse the environment. She loves it when you treat animals and plants with care, love, and respect. Here's a good prayer to say to her:

> *Most Divine Ariel,*
>
> *I ask that you bless this planet with your divine energies.*
>
> *Let your blessings fall on all, living and nonliving.*
>
> *Show me what I need to do to better the world*

and heal this wonderful home called earth.

Thank you.

Help with Animals

Ariel loves animals. She's always ready to heal and help them out, whether they're tame or wild, creatures of the land, sea, or air. If you have a pet that needs to be healed of illness or injury, you can reach out to her for help, and she will be there for them. You can say this prayer:

Most Divine Ariel,

I seek your help. Please keep all the animals safe.

Heal the ones who need healing.

Let your pink healing light encompass them,

refresh them and make them whole again.

I ask that Michael and Raphael work with you

to keep them safe, heal and shield and feed and water them.

Thank you.

For healing

Pray the following incantation:

Most Divine Ariel,

I seek your help. I ask that you heal this (name of creature here).

Heal it from its suffering and pain.

Please work with Raphael to heal this creature,

and encompass it with your loving divine light.

Thank you.

Keeping Animals from Cruelty

Say this prayer:

> *Most Divine Ariel,*
>
> *Please protect these creatures.*
>
> *Keep them safe from cruelty,*
>
> *whether from other animals or humans.*
>
> *Let only love be their lot.*
>
> *Work with Michael to protect them from all danger and cruelty,*
>
> *now and always. Thank you.*

Prayer for Prosperity

If you want to move forward in life, say this prayer to Ariel:

> *Most Divine Ariel,*
>
> *You are the angel of manifestation.*
>
> *I ask that you shower your blessings on me.*
>
> *Let your blessings rain on me and my loved ones.*
>
> *Prosper us financially.*
>
> *Let us live a life of luxury that allows us to do charity.*
>
> *Bless us abundantly that we continue to thrive and prosper.*
>
> *This or better, thank you.*

Prayer for Work and Business

You can ask Ariel to bless your business so that it thrives and prospers. Here's how to pray for that:

> *Most Divine Ariel,*
>
> *I ask that you bless my (name/type of the business)*
>
> *Let your divine energies radiate all over it.*
>
> *Charge this business of mine with financial abundance.*
>
> *Bring me a stream of clients and sales.*

Let my profit continue to grow exponentially.

Bless me with ideas that will let me pull in more profits.

Bless my entire chain of supply.

Show me new ways to make my clients happy.

Send the right clients my way, that we both enjoy

a mutually beneficial relationship.

Bless my business with lots of wonderful reviews

online and by word of mouth.

This or better. Thank you.

Working with Archangel Azrael

Azrael is the angel of transformation who helps souls cross to the other side. He also transforms negative to positive and dark to light. You can call on him when you're dealing with a transition to the afterlife or when you want to change jobs, go into a new career, start a new phase of your life, or change the way you think about things. He seeks to help people move mentally, physically, and emotionally from a place of disconnect to complete wholeness.

Taking Loved Ones to the Other Side

If you're afraid of death, you can reach out to Azrael to quiet those fears. The truth is death feels scary because most people are either worried about going to some dark place after death or no longer existing. Azrael can help you see that death isn't an end – but a *new beginning.* It is like walking through a door out of one room and into another. If a loved one is dying, you can invoke Azrael to help comfort them and make them feel safe.

He usually shows up on his own, and you can tell from the golden-cream light that shows up for the soul that's transitioning. While he's known for leading those who pass on, that's not his only task. Some people pass on, but their spirits remain earthbound. It is Azrael's job to help them move on to the light. If you ever have to deal with earthbound spirits and you're afraid of them, you should call on Azrael to help you. You don't have to be afraid, but you can call him if you can't get over your fear.

Here's a good prayer you can use when dealing with loss and grief:

Archangel Azrael,

I want to thank you for your help with those who are dying.

Thank you for comforting their loved ones who grieve.

As I think about the ones I love who have passed on

and how much I miss them,

please give me comfort in this time of grief.

Help me so that I can heal from this pain

caused by their absence from my life.

Help me to believe in God anew

each time I think of my loved one.

Comfort and assure me that we will be together once again

when it comes my time to leave this world.

When that time comes,

please give me the courage to move on fearlessly.

Fuel me with fire to create a legacy

that's worth leaving behind for when I'm gone.

I ask that in some way, I make the world a better place

by virtue of having been in it.

So that I may feel at peace with my choices

as I breathe my last.

Help me to always remember that I'm never alone.

Remind me that angels are ever with me

as I move through life, and even at the moment of my death.

Amen.

Transmuting Emotional Pain into Wholeness

Do you feel sad and disappointed about something? One way to work with Azrael to heal your pain is to imagine a golden-creamed hue of white light all around you, then ask him to help you look at the situation differently. After making this request, remain in silence for a while, waiting for an answer. You will notice that positive perspectives and images will start to flow through your mind so that you can find the good even in the bad. You might find you are inspired with ideas on tools and resources that will help you work through your emotions, or someone can come to you with the perfect message to help you get through it all. Azrael reminds humanity that the light of God shines within us all. So, if you reach within you, you can tap into his never-ending love and wisdom.

Transforming the Darkness in Your Life to Light

Do you find yourself constantly surrounded by toxic people? Do they wallow and complain a lot? Do they constantly interrupt you and keep you from speaking your truth? There are times when life hits us hard with something, and depending on what we choose to focus on, life can get dark. In times like these, you can invoke Azrael to come to you, your family, or any person or situation that could use some light in place of darkness. As Azrael is adept at turning darkness into light, he can work with those whose energy fields or auras are murky or scattered and help them align with love and truth. Do you have trouble focusing because you're going through tough situations? Or are you unable to commit to your projects until the end? Azrael can help you eliminate all low energy and ego blocks that keep you stuck and distracted. If you're sick and tired of unnecessary drama and useless arguments, and you want to rise above all of that, then you should go to Azrael.

Coping with Changes

Change can be scary and stressful. As humans, we're naturally wired to seek stability. We like when things remain the way they are. The trouble is there can be no growth or development in a world without change. Everything would become meaningless. Change is necessary and a good thing. If you're having trouble accepting the changes that are coming your way, say this prayer to Azrael:

Most Mighty Archangel Azrael,

Please help me learn more about the good plans

that God has for my life.

Let me in on the blueprint for my destiny,

and give me the fire I need in my heart

to pursue this grand goal by getting clear on my priorities

and making the right decisions.

Please help me change all aspects of my life

so that I may be in alignment with what matters most.

When changes happen in my life, and I feel stressed,

please help me to find courage. Help me to understand that

within every challenge is a lesson and a blessing.

Gently remind me that God knows all and sees all,

and he would only ever let me go through

things that will ultimately lead to my good.

Help me keep my heart and mind open

that I may be transformed in every way that God

knows will lead to my growth.

Give me strength and inspiration to

assist others on my path who are experiencing

major changes and who could use some support as they are transformed.

Amen.

Understanding Azrael's Guidance

When you ask for Azrael's help transforming your life, you should know that he will lead you to things that will accelerate your growth. Sometimes, those things might feel a bit uncomfortable, but remember that he means well and that you're not going through it alone. Everything that happens will lead to your ultimate transformation.

The path he takes you down won't always be straight, as is the case with the guidance angels give. It could feel cyclical. You may receive guidance in one aspect of your life, only for that same guidance applies to another seemingly unrelated part of your life.

If your life is imbalanced in one way, that imbalance may cause a ripple effect in other parts of your life that seem to share nothing with the troubled part of your life. But the fact is that your angels can see the connections better than you do. The best thing you can do is to trust Azrael. Believe that he knows what he's doing and knows better than you what you need. You may learn about medicines, books, herbs, oils, classes, and people who can help you with the change you seek along your transformation journey. All these things will happen for you in divine timing.

You need to know that not all angelic advice will come from the process of meditation. Sometimes you can just get an intuitive nudge to say yes to something. For instance, just a few paragraphs before this one, a friend invited me to talk on Zoom. I told her I had a deadline to beat and could only spare about 30 minutes. Well, that call took the better part of two hours, but I don't regret it one bit.

Earlier in the day, I asked for guidance and clarity from Azrael over some changes I've been going through lately and was afraid and full of questions. Without my prompting, the conversation we had veered from work to life in general, and I began to receive clear and precise answers related to what I'd been worried about. After that call, I had to take a moment and thank Azrael for gently nudging me to stay on that call for more than 30 minutes. You see, if I hadn't listened to him, that conversation would have happened without me, and I would have missed out on a lot.

Chapter Twelve: How to Contact Other Spirit Guides

This chapter will focus on tips you need to know to contact your other spirit guides besides angels and archangels.

Be clear in your requests. You need to be certain of what you want. Remember that there's no such thing as too big or too small for your spirit guides. Nothing is too weird either, but it matters that you think about what you really want and be clear about it with them.

Ask them to come to you in your dreams. Dreams are awesome! They create a world where humans and spirits can connect. You can ask your spirit guides to show up in your dreams. You may have already met them before, but you didn't recognize them. However, once you ask them to, they will show up. To ask them, simply take a few moments before bed to say hello, state what it is you'd like help with, and then let them know you'll be expecting them. Don't worry if they don't show up that first night or if you don't remember what was shared with you. They will show up eventually, and if you don't remember what they taught you, you can ask them to show you again and help you remember the next time.

Suppose you're not yet ready to fall asleep after inviting them to your dream. In that case, you can spend time thinking about the situation you want your guides' insight on. You could also read about it so that it is the last thing on your mind before moving your consciousness to the dream world.

I tend to meet my guides in my dreams a lot when I'm learning something new. Often, I find myself walking with someone dressed in ancient robes of purple or deep blue or white. As we walk together, or sometimes just lock eyes with each other, I receive what I can only call blocks of thought from them on whatever it is I'm learning in my waking life.

Sometimes, they'll show me writing on a wall that I can somehow translate to English in my mind. It helps to have a notepad handy by my bed so that as soon as I wake up, I can write down what I received from them in those downloads. Other times, I may not have much clarity on what was shared with me. Still, when I remain in bed with my eyes shut for a few moments, inspiration and insight come to me due to what they taught me in the dream. Sometimes what I learn isn't necessarily about a topic but about a situation in my life and how to resolve it.

Seek a physical sign. You can ask these guides to give you an undeniable sign. It could be an animal, pennies, a feather, or someone talking to you about something that's bothered you. The sign will let you know that your guide truly is with you, has heard you, and is working to bring you what you desire.

Meditate regularly. I can't stress enough how important this is. I'd begun meditating as a teenager only because I'd heard it could help with lucid dreams and astral projection, but the side effects have been wonderful. This practice has opened me up greatly to the spirit world. Now, I can easily communicate with my guides without needing too much time to "get there" or needing ceremonies or rituals. Meditation makes you constantly aware of the world beyond the physical that announces itself in the subtlest of ways.

Also, your guide can reach out to you during mediation. You might see them. Usually, I connect with my guides visually through dreams and out-of-body experiences. Still, there was one time I sat in meditation, chanting HU with my eyes shut. I'd been at it for about fifteen minutes when I saw an old Black man standing before me, with hair and a cropped beard, both stark white. He had a blue and red two-piece toga on. He leaned forward and touched my forehead, right where my third eye is. My eyes flew open since that was the first time I had ever had an experience like that. I knew I didn't imagine things because I could still feel where he had touched me. That night, I had some of the most profound dreams I've ever had.

Make sure you remain unattached to the outcome. In my earlier days, when I'd just become aware of spirit guides, I wanted them to do all kinds of things just to show me they were with me. "Make that table levitate." "Make the power go out." Well, they delivered on the latter, but I'm sad to report that I had no levitating tables around me. I'd figured if I downgraded from a table to a carpet, they might oblige me a la Aladdin's magic carpet, but that didn't happen either. We're still negotiating.

On a serious note, I learned that it was important to release all thoughts of what contacting and communicating with my guides should look like. After all, they are my guides, so why not let them show me the best ways for us to stay in touch with each other? The more I was able to let go and trust them, the easier it was for them to reach out to me and me to them, and the deeper and richer our relationship grew. If you have any expectations of what a guide should look like or do or be, just let all that go and see the unique ways they connect with you. All you have to do is stay open.

Attune your mind to their frequency. For many people, it is not easy to reach out to spirit guides without first setting the mood and getting in the correct headspace. If you're just starting a relationship with them, don't expect that you'll be able to chat as easily as you do with your mates over some beer or wine. You must make sure that you're in alignment with them. That means you will have to meditate regularly, and each time you do, be explicit about your desire to connect with them. This is different from regular meditation, as the intention here is not just to raise your vibration but to let your guides know that you're knocking on their door.

Create a box for questions you have for them. You can use any box or container that feels special to you. Write whatever you want to ask them or whatever is bothering you. Fold it towards you, and then drop it into the box with the assumption that once something goes in the box, you're going to eventually have an answer. This works tremendously well.

Try intuitive writing. This is another great way to connect with your guides and learn what they have to say. You start by clearing out a sacred space or corner of your room or home. You can burn some incense or sage to clear the energies of that space. Then light a candle and sit with your pen and journal in hand. Take a few deep breaths and relax. Allow your hand with the pen to rest on the journal, relaxed yet ready to write. You can begin by writing a question and then waiting. When you feel moved, allow your hand to begin writing across the page. Don't think about what's coming through you. Just let it flow easily, and don't try to analyze it or judge it as you write. When you're done, you'll know it because you'll begin to pause in between words. Stop there and then. If you have other questions, you can take a few grounding breaths, write the next question, and allow your hand to move as directed by your guides again.

Summon your team. A good way to get in touch with your guides is by calling on them just to say hello. Another good time to summon them is when you need some divine help with something you are working on. Say you're writing your first book. You could call on a guide who has experience writing their own stuff and ask them to assist you in figuring out your message or the plot. When I plan a new book and feel a little lost, I happily summon my divine writing team.

Every time I do, I churn out amazing stuff, thanks to their help. I don't think they know what writer's block means, I'd say.

Don't be a micromanager. If you want to connect with your guides, you shouldn't attempt to control everything they do. Trust that whatever you've asked them for, they will deliver. Give them room to work on your behalf. Allow them the time to answer you. Usually, their timing is very stellar, so you'd be better off relaxing rather than questioning their capabilities.

Keep a diary. This diary should have every detail about your spirit guides in it. When you have guidance or help from them in the form of dreams, visions, or intuitive hunches, you should write them down. This way, you can look back on them and track your progress in your relationship with your guides. It helps to have a solid record of how often their advice works out in your favor. Also, note the negative repercussions that come from refusing to listen to them, if any. This diary will serve as empirical evidence that your guides are very real, know what they're doing, and should be reached out to and always trusted.

Spirit Guide Meditation

Find somewhere quiet and comfortable. It would help if this place is somewhere you can return to every day to meditate. You should make sure you're wearing a loose, comfortable outfit. Turn off every electrical device that might distract you. Sit down in a comfortable position and shut your eyes. Start to notice your breath. Breathe in deep and slow through your nose, and then exhale through your slightly parted lips. Continue to breathe this way, remaining in the moment. Allow all the chatter in your mind to drain away. If you get distracted, be glad you noticed, and lovingly return to focusing on your breath. As you exhale, allow all the tension in your body to drain out completely. When you feel fully relaxed, envision somewhere peaceful, beautiful, and outside. You can go to any place that makes you feel the most relaxed, happy, and sage.

As your guides are subtle in reaching out to you, you should spend this time asking them to make themselves known to you. You can make this request out loud or in your mind. Even if this seems foolish to you, don't feel that way. Be patient and continue to ask them.

When you're deeply relaxed, you may get visions or images in your head. Keep your attention on them. Keep your breath at the same relaxed pace, in through your nose and out through your mouth. Imagine that your inhales pull in positive energies and lift your vibration to line up with those of your spirit guides.

Do the images in your head resemble someone female or male? Are they clear? When you get a clear vision, you should ask them what their name is, or you can just ask for their help with whatever issue you need guidance on. Expect that you will receive an intuitive nudge or some other sign from them. If they're not, don't let this frustrate you. Notice if you can feel a change in the temperature around you, someone touching you, movement in the air, or some warmth.

The key to successfully contacting your guides is to continue trying with confidence that they will reach out to you. It may take a week, a day, or longer, but don't quit on them. Always show them you're thankful when they assist you.

Know that your guides might not necessarily communicate with you through spoken words. They might use subtle means, a dream, vision, or a favorite song that suddenly comes on. You might suddenly find something you've been looking for. Also, the messages you receive might not make sense to you initially, but as time passes, you will begin to make sense of them.

The closer you become to your guides, the more information you'll get on whatever you want. They'll let you know why they've been watching you and what you need to do to get to where you want to be in life. You will notice that your dreams are clearer and last longer. You might also begin experiencing things like spontaneous astral projections, premonitions, prophecy, healing, and so on.

Communicating with Other Spirits with Your Guides' Protection

When you finally access the spirit realm, it can be such a thrill. You get to learn and explore so much more than the mundane things that happen here on earth. That said, you should always go with the awareness that your guides are with you. The spirit realm is full of the unknown, and not all of it is necessarily good for you. Therefore, you should make a point of connecting with your guides before you try reaching out to other spirits. Your guides are always with you. However, consciously asking them to protect you will strengthen the protection you already have from them. It will also keep you calm and at ease as you explore the mysteries of the world.

So, when you want to interact with any spirit that isn't necessarily affiliated to you, here's the way to do it while being safe:

First, boost your protection. Before you begin knocking on spiritual doors or inviting spirits to your space, you should work on keeping your energy and space safe by meditating. In your meditation, envision a brilliant, bright white light that encompasses your whole self. Then call upon your guides to amplify the protection of this light and to keep you safe from all that wish you ill. You can also make use of amethyst, as it has protective qualities. Simply wearing it around your neck as jewelry will do.

Sanctify a space. You want to create a space that is meant only for spirit interactions. You can sanctify it by saging it and keeping it free of clutter. Remove all things that would serve as a distraction. You can also place herbs, plants, crystals, and candles around the space to improve the ambiance. Also, get a pen and paper ready to record your experiences and what you learn.

Clarify your intention. When you're in this sacred space, make your intentions known and clear. Also, be clear about the sort of experiences you're open to having and set boundaries about the only kinds of spirits you will entertain. If you know who you're trying to connect with, you could say, "I intend to connect with (name of person or spirit). Dear guides, please keep an eye on me, guide and protect me, and make it so that the messages I receive come from only this person. Let me receive the message lovingly and gently. Keep me safe all through this process and help me gain only what is good for me."

If you're not sure that the spirit you want to reach out to is good, you can tell your guides to gatekeep the entire interaction so that you remain safe all through. Do this when you're working with spirits you do not know, especially if it is your first time. When it comes to unknown spirits, don't be quick to interact with them. First, take the time to check out their energy. Are you picking up on bad vibes? Or are you not sure about what their intention is? Ask your guides to remove the spirit. Then end the session. Or you could leave that process to an expert. Make sure you sage your home if you weren't sure about the spirit you invited.

If you feel afraid, that's not the best time to reach out to the spirit world. You should only attempt to do so when you feel up to it and can keep your mind clear.

Stay open to what you receive. Once you've set your intention and figured out that the spirit is alright, you can address it and ask whatever you want. Then wait for them to answer. Sometimes the answers might come in flashes of light, tingles, other sensations, synchronicity, and even audible messages. Write down anything you feel and get. Understand you may not get an immediate answer, or it might not be as clear as you'd like. Just keep your mind open and trust that you'll understand them.

Shut the door. When you're done with your questions, wrap up your session by declaring you're done. You can send the spirit on its way by saying goodbye. Remember to also thank it for the message it had for you. Once you're done, use sage to clear out all residual aura from the spirits and cleanse your space. You can use any other cleansing incense and ring some bells as well. As you cleanse the space, declare aloud, "I cleanse this space and keep it protected with love and light, only love and light may flourish here." Please shut the door and cleanse your space even when you feel you didn't successfully connect with any spirit.

Conclusion

We have finally come to the end of this book, and I am certain that you've learned a lot about reaching out to your wonderful guardians and archangels. Now the rest of it is up to you. Are you going to let all you've learned go to waste, or are you going to establish a deeper relationship between yourself and your guardians?

You may have read this book just out of curiosity. Your life may be a wonderful one already. If that's the case, great! However, your life could become even more magical if you decide here and now to say hello to your wonderful angels.

If you've been going through a lot and could really use some support, love, and assistance in your life, call on your angels. Do you feel lost? Tired? Like you've spent too much time and energy spinning around in circles, and you have nothing to show for it? Then you should absolutely reach out to them. Give them full permission to help you and see how your life turns around for the better.

We weren't supposed to go through life with absolutely no support from divinity at all. Think about it: Would you send your kids off somewhere to be on their own without a babysitter? So why would the Source of all life, the ultimate Divine Being, leave us to our devices on this not-so-little blue dot? You have a team of angels ready and willing to assist you through whatever struggles you may be going through. You could stubbornly go about it on your own, and they would only help you as much as they can without infringing on your free will. But once you call on them and give them the green light, nothing in your life will remain the same. You'll wonder how on earth you could have allowed yourself to live so long without the love and guidance of these amazing, beautiful beings.

Here's another book by Mari Silva that you might like

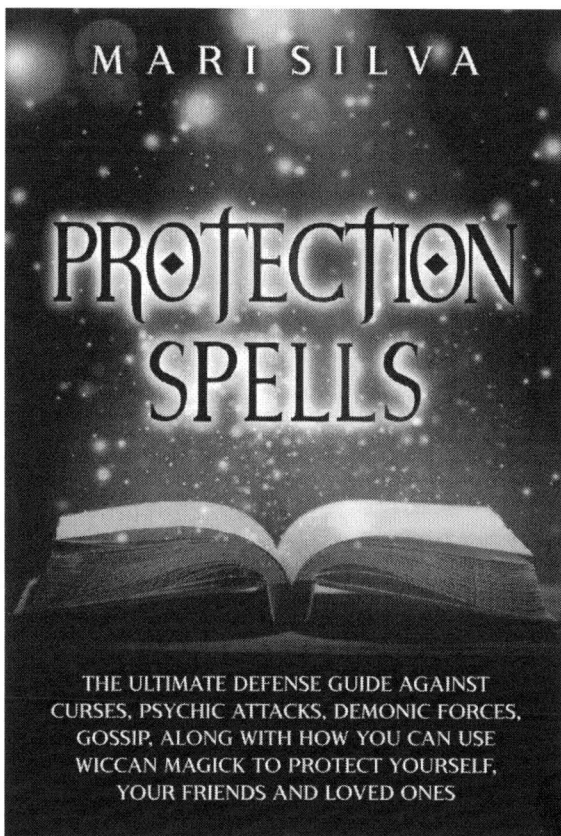

MARI SILVA

PROTECTION SPELLS

THE ULTIMATE DEFENSE GUIDE AGAINST
CURSES, PSYCHIC ATTACKS, DEMONIC FORCES,
GOSSIP, ALONG WITH HOW YOU CAN USE
WICCAN MAGICK TO PROTECT YOURSELF,
YOUR FRIENDS AND LOVED ONES

Your Free Gift (only available for a limited time)

Thanks for getting this book! If you want to learn more about various spirituality topics, then join Mari Silva's community and get a free guided meditation MP3 for awakening your third eye. This guided meditation mp3 is designed to open and strengthen ones third eye so you can experience a higher state of consciousness. Simply visit the link below the image to get started.

https://spiritualityspot.com/meditation

References

Armentrout, Don S. (1 January 2000). An Episcopal Dictionary of the Church. Church Publishing, Inc.

Boyce, Mary (1984). Textual Sources for the Study of Zoroastrianism. Manchester, UK: Manchester University Press.

Bamberger, Bernard Jacob, (15 March 2006). Fallen Angels: Soldiers of Satan's Realm. Jewish Publication Society of America.

Barker, Margaret (2004). An Extraordinary Gathering of Angels, M Q Publications.

Bennett, William Henry (1911), "Angel," in Chisholm, Hugh (ed.), Encyclopædia Britannica, 2 (11th ed.), Cambridge University Press.

Briggs, Constance Victoria, 1997. The Encyclopedia of Angels: An A-to-Z Guide with Nearly 4,000 Entries. Plume.

Bunson, Matthew, (1996). Angels A to Z: A Who's Who of the Heavenly Host. Three Rivers Press.

Cheyne, James Kelly (ed.) (1899). Angel. Encyclopædia Biblica. New York, Macmillan.

Driver, Samuel Rolles (Ed.) (1901) The book of Daniel. Cambridge UP.

Graham, Billy, 1994. Angels: God's Secret Agents. W Pub Group; Minibook edition. Guiley, Rosemary, 1996. Encyclopedia of Angels.

Jastrow, Marcus, 1996, A Dictionary of the Targumim, the Talmud Bavli and Yerushalmi, and the Midrashic literature compiled by Marcus Jastrow, PhD., Litt.D. with an index of Scriptural quotations, Vol 1 & 2, The Judaica Press, New York

Kainz, Howard P., "Active and Passive Potency" in Thomistic Angelology Martinus Nijhoff.

Kreeft, Peter J. 1995. Angels and Demons: What Do We Really Know About Them? Ignatius Press.

Lewis, James R. (1995). Angels A to Z. Visible Ink Press.

Melville, Francis, 2001. The Book of Angels: Turn to Your Angels for Guidance, Comfort, and Inspiration. Barron's Educational Series; 1st edition.

Noegel, Scott B.; Wheeler, Brannon M. (2002). Historical Dictionary of Prophets in Islam and Judaism. Scarecrow Press

Printed in Great Britain
by Amazon